HOW TO READ
EXODUS

TREMPER LONGMAN III

IVP Academic
An imprint of InterVarsity Press
Downers Grove, Illinois

InterVarsity Press
P.O. Box 1400, Downers Grove, IL 60515-1426
World Wide Web: www.ivpress.com
E-mail: email@ivpress.com

InterVarsity Press® is the book-publishing division of InterVarsity Christian Fellowship/USA®, a
movement of students and faculty active on campus at hundreds of universities, colleges and schools of
nursing in the United States of America, and a member movement of the International Fellowship of
Evangelical Students. For information about local and regional activities, write Public Relations Dept.,
InterVarsity Christian Fellowship/USA, 6400 Schroeder Rd., P.O. Box 7895, Madison, WI 53707-7895,
or visit the IVCF website at <www.intervarsity.org>.

Unless otherwise indicated, all Scripture quotations are taken from the Holy Bible, New Living
Translation, copyright ©1996, 2004. Used by permission of Tyndale House Publishers, Inc., Wheaton,
Illinois 60189. All rights reserved.

Design: Kathy Burrows

Images: Illustration of a camp, Roberta Polfus

ISBN 978-0-8308-3858-5

Printed in the United States of America ∞

Library of Congress Cataloging-in-Publication Data

Longman, Tremper.
   How to read Exodus / Tremper Longman III.
      p. cm.
   Includes bibliographical references and index.
   ISBN 978-0-8308-3858-5 (pbk.: alk. paper)
   1. Bible. O.T. Exodus—Criticism, interpretation, etc. I. Title.
BS1245.52.L66 2009
222'.12061—dc22

                                                                                2009021523

P   23 22 21 20 19 18 17 16 15 14 13 12 11 10 9 8 7 6 5 4 3 2

Y   28 27 26 25 24 23 22 21 20 19 18 17 16 15 14 13

CONTENTS

1

READING EXODUS
WITH A STRATEGY

■   ■   ■

Today Christians typically pay more attention to Genesis than to Exodus. A partial explanation for this situation can be found in the incredible focus often paid to the question of creation, which has fed a "culture war" between those who believe God created the world and those who don't. Another contributing factor is simply the fact that Genesis is the first book in the canon (the body of writings the church recognizes as the standard of its faith and its practice).

Without a doubt, Genesis is an important book, providing the foundation to much that follows. It deserves close study. That said, in its ancient context it is the preface to the book of Exodus. To be more exact, we must remember that the first five books of the Bible (Genesis through

Deuteronomy) are really a single literary whole that goes by various names: The Book of Moses, the Torah and the Pentateuch. Genesis is the introduction to the real focus of the Torah, the founding of Israel as a nation. Thus, the book of Exodus assumes tremendous significance as it describes how Israel escaped its captivity in Egypt, received the law that defined it as a nation, and built a central worship site, the Tabernacle. Genesis provides a background to prepare the reader for hearing the story of the Exodus.

How to Read Exodus gives a roadmap for interpreting this important book. It is the fourth book in a series that includes *How to Read Psalms*, *How to Read Proverbs* and *How to Read Genesis*. These are not commentaries on the books, but guides to interpretive strategies. Even so, *How to Read Exodus* chapters seven through nine will provide an overview of the contents of the book in the light of the background provided in the other chapters. In chapters ten through twelve, we will explore the continuing impact that the book of Exodus has on subsequent biblical revelation, both in the Old and the New Testament.

The next, introductory chapter will provide an overview of interpretive principles that are important for the study of Exodus. These principles will sound familiar to those who have read my previous book on Genesis. Genesis and Exodus are similar in genre (compared to Psalms and Proverbs, the other books treated thus far in this series), and so many of the ideas in chapter one of *How to Read Genesis* will be repeated here. However, the examples will come from Exodus rather than from Genesis. For those who have already read *How to Read Genesis*, reading the next chapter will provide helpful review and preparation for the rest of the book.

WHAT IS THE PURPOSE OF INTERPRETATION ANYWAY?

In our modern/postmodern world, people have divergent views of the purpose of interpretation. The question of the purpose of interpretation is integrally related to the issue of the location of the meaning of a text. It makes a world of difference whether one believes that the meaning of a text is identified with the intended message of the author or not. Most readers assume that their interpretation of a text replicates the meaning of the author. Contemporary literary theory, however, has questioned whether such a goal is even possible.[1] After all, readers typically do not have direct access to authors, but rather are restricted to the words on the page. How can we know for sure that our understanding of the text faithfully reproduces that of the author? Indeed, even if the author was present and we could ask him or her questions, we may still have problems. Perhaps authors wrote better than they knew or have forgotten what they meant by their words.

Of course, with the book of Exodus such problems are deeply compounded. In the first place, the author is dead. In the second place, since Exodus is an anonymous composition we cannot be absolutely certain who wrote different parts of the book. Even if we end up agreeing with the traditional authorship ascription to Moses, we cannot believe he wrote every word of it (see appendix 1). But even granting Moses wrote the entirety of Exodus, those of us who believe in the divine inspiration of the book have yet a further complication. When we talk about the author's intention, are we referring to the human or the divine author's intention? Some try to guard against this problem by insisting that the human author was fully conscious of the divine intention in the writing.[2] However, the New Testament claims that the prophets spoke better than they knew (1 Pet 1:10-12), and we would be very hard pressed to believe that the human authors of the Old Testament would have known all the interpretive meaning that the New Testament authors recognized in their writings (as when Matthew cites the exodus tradition of Hosea 11; see chapter 9).[3]

---

[1]See Tremper Longman III, "Literary Approaches to Biblical Interpretation," in *Foundations of Contemporary Interpretation,* ed. Moisés Silva (Grand Rapids: Zondervan, 1996), pp. 103-23. See also D. Firth and J. Grant, eds., *Words and the Word: Explorations in Biblical Interpretation and Literary Theory* (Downers Grove, Ill.: InterVarsity Press, 2008).

[2]See Walter Kaiser, "The Meaning of Meaning," in *An Introduction to Biblical Hermeneutics,* by Walter Kaiser and Moisés Silva (Grand Rapids: Zondervan, 1994), pp. 27-44.

[3]See the helpful discussion of New Testament quotations of Old Testament texts in Peter Enns, *Inspiration and Incarnation: Evangelicals and the Problem of the Old Testament* (Grand Rapids: Baker, 2005), pp. 113-66.

Such issues lead many readers to abandon the language of authorial intention and move to a text-based interpretive method. They feel more comfortable talking in terms of what the text says as opposed to what an author meant by a particular passage. Such a strategy helpfully concentrates focus on the literary conventions of the text, particularly genre (see below). On the other hand, study of the text does not have to result in the abandonment of the goal of discovering the author's intention. While reminding us that our only access to the author's mind is through the text, we can still speak in terms of discovering the author's intention in the literary conventions of the text, or at least make a hypothesis about the author's meaning.

Finally, some interpreters go so far as to completely deny that a literary/biblical text has a determinate meaning.[4] A passage only means what the reader says that it means. In reaction to this idea, we should not ignore the fact that readers play a major role in the specific interpretation of a text. Readers approach a text with certain lenses formed by their gender and their economic, ethnic and theological background.[5] We are finite beings that cannot fully grasp the meaning of a text as rich as Exodus. The involvement of the reader in the interpretation of the text is also enhanced when we realize that interpretation should be understood as more than what the text meant to the original audience but what it means to us today.

Again, we should affirm the role of the reader in the determination of the meaning. We should accordingly expand our interpretation and correct its distortions by reading with a community of readers who will attend to different aspects of the text. Even so, some reader-response critics understand the reader's role even more radically. They do not allow their interpretation to be shaped by the text at all. Indeed, some (deconstructionists) exert their "interpretive" energy to undermine the

---

[4]See D. J. A. Clines, "A World Established on Water (Psalm 24): Reader-Response, Deconstruction, and Bespoke Criticism," in *The New Literary Criticism and the Hebrew Bible*, ed. J. C. Exum and D. J. A. Clines (JSOTSup 143; Sheffield: Sheffield Academic Press, 1993), pp. 79-90.
[5]See Tremper Longman III, *Reading the Bible with Heart and Mind* (Colorado Springs, Colo.: NavPress, 1997), pp. 61-68.

idea that the text communicates any meaning at all.

In the final analysis, the best understanding of the purpose of interpretation is to understand that our goal is to rediscover the message of the author. We do so tempered by the understanding that we have access to the author only through the text, so to understand the text of Exodus, we should study the conventions of Hebrew narrative and law. Our reading should also be humbled by recognition that our final interpretation is a hypothesis about the author's meaning.[6] The most important parts of an author's message are said so often and in so many different ways that it is hard to misconstrue them (unless one is a purposefully mischievous reader). However, not everything in the text is equally important and interpreters must exercise humility in the way in which they present their interpretive conclusions.

---

[6]G. Strickland, *Structuralism or Criticism? Thoughts on How We Read* (Cambridge: Cambridge University Press, 1981).

ONE

UNDERSTANDING THE
BOOK OF "DEPARTURE"

WHY NOT JUST READ THE BOOK AND NOT WORRY ABOUT PRINCIPLES OR STUDY?

Many readers of the Bible worry that the study of interpretive principles (hermeneutics) actually hinders the proper appropriation of its message. Since we believe that the message ultimately comes from God himself, study can get in the way of our communion with God. In other words, if we engage our mind, it short circuits our heart's engagement with God through his Word.

It would be wrong of me to deny that this is a danger of academic study of the Bible. There are too many living examples of people who are excellent students of the Word but have a dead faith. However, the two are not mutually exclusive.[1]

The truth of the matter is that the Bible is not an easy book to understand. The basic message is clear, but many of the details are matters of disagreement. To avoid reading into the message whatever we want, we

---

[1]My book *Reading the Bible with Heart and Mind* (Colorado Springs, Colo.: NavPress, 1997) attempts to navigate a way through an approach to the reading of the Bible that engages both heart and mind.

need to discipline our study by observing certain principles that can help guide us to a proper interpretation of its meaning.

One of the main reasons why the Bible, and in particular the book of Exodus, is difficult to understand is because it is a book from a different age and a different culture. Most of the people reading my book are from a Western (or perhaps Westernized) culture and everyone (unless this book has an amazing shelf life!) is from the twenty-first century A.D. The book of Exodus is from a Near Eastern culture rooted in the second millennium B.C. Many of the principles that follow in this chapter are specifically intended to help us bridge the gap between the second millennium B.C. and the third millennium A.D. They address questions of historical background and ancient Near Eastern context. They ask questions about the literary conventions (genre, outline, style, narrative structure) of ancient Israel. If we try to read the book of Exodus as if it were written in our time, then we will misunderstand it.

On the surface of it, it is obvious that most people cannot simply sit down and read the book of Exodus without doing serious study. Remember that part of its historical distance from us is the fact that it is written in ancient Hebrew. To even read it at all, the text has to be translated into a modern language like English. Many lay readers forget about this fact since the Bible is available in so many English versions, some of which make the text sound as if it were written yesterday. By the time most people sit down to read the book of Exodus, thousands upon thousands of hours of scholarly work have been spent rendering it into English.

However, speaking of principles, we must not err in the other direction either. It is not possible to give a specific set of principles that can lead us to a clear and inerrant interpretation. Interpretation is more like an art than a science. We need to be mindful of principles like the ones mentioned below, but we must apply them like an artist and not a scientist. They are guidelines not rigid rules.

Finally, and most importantly, prayer is more important than principles. God speaks to us through his Word, and we speak to him through prayer. The Bible is not an ancient manuscript that needs to be dissected by objective readers, it is a message of love and guidance from our heavenly Father who not only speaks to us through its pages, but also sends the Holy Spirit to guide us in our reading. We must put ourselves under and not over the Word, and prayer puts us in the proper attitude of submission as we interpret. Psalm 119:18 ("Open my eyes to see the wonderful truths in your instructions") provides a model for such a prayerful attitude. Let's approach the following discussion together in such an attitude of prayer.

PRINCIPLE 1: RECOGNIZE THE LITERARY NATURE OF THE BOOK OF EXODUS

As a part of the Bible, most readers, lay and clergy, approach the book of Exodus for its teaching about God and his relationship with his people (theology). Since the first part of the book (Ex 1–15) tells the dramatic story of Israel's rescue from Egypt, historical questions also occupy our attention. These concerns and interests are right and important (see below), but as we read the book for these purposes we must bear in mind that Exodus is also a literary composition. As such, we need to address literary questions as we explore its theology and history, otherwise we may misunderstand what the author (see above) intends to teach us about God's actions in history.

Literary issues include the genre, style, composition and structure of the book. The following questions introduce us to these concerns in anticipation of applications and descriptions of the book of Exodus in the chapters that follow.

Question 1: What kind of book is Exodus? In other words, what is its genre or literary type? Genre triggers reading strategy. If a literary composition begins "once upon a time," then readers will take the words that follow as a fairy tale rather than a scientific essay. "Once upon a time" is a generic signal used by an author to communicate to readers the type of purpose he or she has in writing.

Modern literature often comes clearly marked in terms of genre. Bookstores and libraries arrange their collections according to genre. Biographies, science fiction, self-help books, travel books, cookbooks will be found in different sections. Title pages may announce that the book is a novel or historical fiction.

Biblical literature, and ancient literature in general, is more problematic in this regard. First, we encounter the books of the Bible in a single collection, leading some to mistakenly believe that all the books belong to a single genre. Of course, even a moment's reflection will reveal that this is a faulty conclusion. Aside from history, the Bible contains law, poetry, wisdom, prophecy, apocalypse and letters. Each of these genres has its own "reading strategy."[2] Second, the books of the Bible are all ancient literature and therefore have differences from modern literature. Ancient history books may be different from modern history textbooks, for instance. Third, since biblical books don't have title pages and ancient authors use different literary conventions than modern authors, modern interpreters have to pay attention to more subtle clues as to the author's signals to readers. Accordingly, we will pay careful attention to the genre(s) of the book of Exodus in chapter two.

Question 2: How did ancient Hebrews tell stories? The book of Exodus, like much of the Old Testament, recounts the past in a story-like fashion. In other words, it is history (see chapters 5-6), but the account of events is given in a vivid, concrete and passionate style. The composer of the story of the exodus pays attention to how he tells the story as well as the message of the account itself.

Accordingly, we should not be surprised that Hebrew narrative, the story of the exodus included, can be described using terms like plot, characterization, narrator and point of view. The account of the exodus is a well-told Hebrew story, and as a Hebrew story it is appropriate to ask the question, how did ancient Hebrews tell stories?

Different cultures tell their stories in different ways. They are not radically different or we would not recognize them as stories or use the categories that we use to describe, say, stories written in English, in our study of Hebrew narrative. Even so, narrators may function differently in stories from different cultures, and characters may be presented in

---

[2]See Gordon Fee and Douglas Stuart, *How to Read the Bible for All Its Worth,* 3rd ed. (Grand Rapids: Zondervan, 2003), and Longman, *Reading the Bible.*

different ways. Understanding the conventions of Hebrew storytelling will guide the reader in proper interpretation.

The interested student can find book-length studies of biblical narrative.[3] At this point, only the most basic features of style can be briefly described. Because of space constraints, only those distinctive features that shape Hebrew narrative will be commented on. For instance, plot, with its traditional beginning, middle and end, is not much different if one is reading the exodus story or, say, *Moby Dick*. Point of view is not different either really. Hebrew narrative is presented by an anonymous and omniscient third-person narrator. Though such a narrative strategy may be seen in literature of other cultures, it is interesting that Hebrew narrative is almost exclusively in this style (an exception may be found in the memoir form of Ezra–Nehemiah). In a book like Exodus that is in the context of the Torah, the third person narrator begins to sound like God himself since he is omniscient, even knowing the thoughts of the characters.

On the other hand, characters are presented somewhat differently from what we may be used to in English literature. First of all, notice that we only know characters like Moses through the lens provided by the narrator who usually does not so much *tell* us about the character as *show* us. And, interestingly, the narrator shows us predominantly through the speech of characters rather than through extensive narrative description of actions. Notice, for instance, just how little physical description we have of the characters. This contrasts sharply, say, with nineteenth-century storytelling (George Eliot novels for instance), which are replete with physical descriptions of the characters. This paucity of physical description alerts us to the fact that when the narrator does choose to say something about how someone looks, say Moses' "shining face" (Ex 34:30), that information is very important.

---

[3]Some of the best are Robert Alter, *The Art of Biblical Narrative* (New York: Basic Books, 1981); M. Sternberg, *The Poetics of Biblical Narrative: Ideological Literature and the Drama of Reading* (Bloomington: Indiana University Press, 1985); and A. Berlin, *Poetics and Interpretation of Biblical Narrative* (Sheffield: Almond, 1983).

There are other ways in which the story chooses to reveal only certain aspects of the character's personality. Notice just how infrequently we learn of motivations for a character's actions. The narrator rarely gives them. And even when a character chooses to do so, we are not always sure they are telling us the truth! Aaron's excuses for making the golden calf are one clear example of this (Ex 32:22-24). Is Aaron confessing or dissimulating? We are often left with many questions.

Awareness of such features of Hebrew storytelling comes with much exposure to the stories themselves as well as studying some of the excellent guides listed in the bibliography at the end of the chapter.

Question 3: Was Exodus written at one time by a single person? Exodus, as we now know it, is not really an individual book, but rather part of a five-part composition known as the Torah (Instruction/Law) or Pentateuch (five scrolls). Genesis was the preamble to the story of the founding of Israel as a nation, an account coterminous with the life of Moses. Accordingly, the issue of the composition of Exodus is part of the larger question of who wrote the Pentateuch.

Considering that neither Exodus nor the Pentateuch names an author, passions have run high on both sides of this question. There are those who believe that Moses wrote it and anyone who disagrees with that viewpoint is theologically suspect. On the other hand, there are those who believe that Moses had nothing to do with the book, and anyone who thinks otherwise is a hopeless fundamentalist.

Certainly, theological issues are at stake in the question. Often those who believe the book was written after the time of Moses argue that the authority of the book does not depend on its human author. The Pentateuch and later Scripture, however, seem to invest Moses with authority as the one who received the law.[4] On the other hand, parts of the Pentateuch were clearly written after the death of Moses (most clearly the account of his death in Deuteronomy 34). Thus, the issue seems to need more nuance than the extreme positions grant it. This issue will be discussed in appendix one.

---

[4]See Ex 24:4; 34:27; Num 33:2; Deut 31:22; Josh 1:7, 8; 2 Chron 25:4; Ezra 6:18; Neh 13:1; Mt 19:7; 22:24; Mk 7:10; 12:26; Jn 1:17; 5:46; 7:23.

Question 4. What can we learn about Exodus from comparable ancient Near Eastern literature? The Bible was not written in a cultural vacuum. God did not create a new language unrelated to any others to communicate his revelation to his people. The book of Exodus is written in Hebrew, related in varying degrees to a number of different Semitic languages. Studying these other, related languages (particularly Ugaritic, Aramaic and Akkadian) helps us understand the meaning of Hebrew words. In the same way, the literary forms of the book of Exodus have analogues in the ancient Near East. Thus, we will find it helpful to read the laws of Exodus 20–23 in the context of ancient Near Eastern law, study the form of the tabernacle in the light of ancient Near Eastern worship places, and much, much more. Such concerns will be dealt with in chapter four.

PRINCIPLE 2: EXPLORE THE HISTORICAL BACKGROUND OF THE BOOK

Readers can recognize immediately the historical interests of the book of Exodus. Its beginning connects with the story of Jacob and his sons in the book of Genesis and how that family found itself in Egypt. It then informs us that in the unstated number of years that followed their numerous descendants found themselves in a completely different situation in that country that at first welcomed them.

The narration continues, telling us about people and events that took place in the past. The book is unmistakably historical in intention. Of course, just because a work purports to be a work of history does not make it a true report. For that reason, it is important to discuss the question of the veracity of its presentation. We will see that Exodus and biblical historiography in general are not interested in history for antiquarian purposes. History is important because it reveals God and his people's relationship to God (theology). Even so, due to its concern for, and the fact that its composition is embedded in, history, the interpreter is moved to ask the book certain questions.

Question 5: When was Exodus written? The question of the historical background begins with the question of when the book was written. If we can determine when it was written we can often come to understand the reason why the book was written, that is, what the author intended to teach his contemporary audience.

Of course, this question is integrally connected with question 3. Was the book written by one person at one period of time or did it come into existence over a longer period of time (appendix 1)?

Question 6: What does Exodus tell us about the past? The answer to this question will depend in great measure on what we determine the genre of the book to be. Does the book intend to tell us anything about the past? However, even if we decide that the book intends to inform its reader about actual events, that does not mean that the book does so well or accurately. As we will see in chapter six, this question is of monumental importance for our appropriation of the book of Exodus.

Question 7: Does our knowledge of the ancient Near East help us understand Exodus? Above in question 4, we considered the importance of studying the Bible in the light of ancient Near Eastern material for literary reasons. A second reason exists for studying the book of Exodus in the light of ancient Near Eastern materials. Biblical religion is a historical religion; it records the acts of God in space and time. The book of Exodus describes events that largely take place in Egypt. We would be remiss not to address the question of how the story of Israel's bondage and eventual freedom from that ancient Near Eastern superpower fits in with what we know from ancient Egyptian sources. We will also take up this matter in chapter six.

PRINCIPLE 3: REFLECT ON THE THEOLOGICAL TEACHING OF THE BOOK.

In the final analysis, the book of Exodus is not just good literature or a record of past events, it reveals God to its readers. Faithful Jewish and Christian readers believe that the book is God's own self-disclosure to his people. While written by human author(s), ultimately God describes his own nature and interprets his own actions in the world. Jewish tradition has acknowledged this by affirming that the Torah, which includes the book of Exodus, "renders the hands unclean,"[5] while Christian theology universally recognizes its canonical status. The following questions aid the reader in discerning how God makes his presence known in the text.

Question 8: How does Exodus describe God? Exodus tells the (hi)story of the deliverance of Israel from its bondage in Egypt, the reception of the law that would govern the emerging nation, and the construction of the tabernacle. One does not have to read deeply to recognize that deliverance, law and tabernacle are the results of God's activity. He rescues his people from Egypt, gives them their law and commands them to build the tabernacle. We clearly see that Exodus describes God in large part through narrating his actions in the real world. Thus, a theology of Exodus will recognize that the book of Exodus is a divine interpretation of the meaning of the historical events it narrates.

But Exodus gives its reader more than divine action. It also describes the divine nature. Of course, there is not a radical divide between his actions and his nature. When he divided the Sea, Israel recognized God as powerful, strong and glorious. Often the book of Exodus pictures God through the use of metaphor. Metaphor teaches about God through comparing him to things with which his people had experience. For instance, also after the crossing of the Sea, Moses called God a "warrior" (Ex 15:3). The sensitive reader will pay attention not just to the narration of God's actions in the book but also to the metaphors that are used to describe who he is.

Question 9: How does Exodus describe God's relationship to his people? From the book of Genesis, we learned that there is only one God and that all other creatures (spiritual, human, animal, inanimate) are his creatures. He made them all. Genesis 1–2 go further and strongly suggest that, while all God's creation is precious to him, human beings occupy a special place in his heart.

---

[5]This terminology sounds strange to Christians unacquainted with the idea that humans are rendered ritually unclean by coming into contact with holy objects. In other words it is the holiness of the book that renders the one who handles the scroll containing the book of Exodus unclean. For more, see Roger Beckwith, *The Old Testament Canon in the New Testament Church* (London: SPCK, 1985), pp. 17, 34, 39, 85-86, 278-81.

Most theologians agree that God is self-sufficient in and of himself. As revelation continues and expands from the Old Testament and into the New Testament, the Trinitarian nature of God becomes increasingly clear. God is one, but he exists in three persons. Theologians thus speak of the fact that God does not need his creatures (a doctrine referred to as the aseity of God).

While it is theologically important to affirm that God is not dependent on his creatures, such a theological dictum occasionally leads to a cold, impersonal, passionless view of God. In other words, the exact opposite of the picture the Bible and a book like Exodus presents to its readers. On the contrary, the Bible, including Exodus, never describes God in the abstract but always in relationship. Indeed, the story of Exodus is the account of God who has bound himself in relationship to his people (covenant) and thus delivers them from their bondage and makes his presence known to them through his law and tabernacle. The radically relational nature of God is also taught through the various metaphors of the book. For instance, the warrior implies an army; it is not just an abstract idea. It is important to remain sensitive to this important aspect of biblical theology as we read the book of Exodus.

Question 10: How does Exodus fit into the whole of Scripture? On the one hand, it would be easy to restrict our study of the book of Exodus to the confines of the book itself. As we have already seen, though, Exodus is part of a larger literary whole, the Pentateuch. While there is a chronological gap between Genesis 50 and Exodus 1, there is no question that Exodus is picking up the story where it ended in Genesis. The end of Genesis anticipated the story of the Exodus when the dying Joseph told his brothers: "God will surely come to help you and lead you out of this land of Egypt. He will bring you back to the land he solemnly promised to give to Abraham, to Isaac, and to Jacob" (Gen 50:24). In the same way that Exodus continues the story of Genesis, so the story continues in Leviticus, Numbers and Deuteronomy. After all, the opening of Exodus tells us about the birth of Moses, while Deuteronomy 34 narrates his death.

However, like Genesis, Deuteronomy concludes with the expectation of the continuation of the story. Moses dies, but the people of God are still on the wrong side of the Jordan River. If God's promises are true, then the narration will continue in the future, and it surely does in the book of Joshua.

Indeed, the book of Exodus is an important part of the story of God's redemption of his people that begins in Genesis and extends into the New Testament. The canon is made up of many books. These books have different emphases and contributions to make to our knowledge of God and our relationship with him. The church's recognition of this collection of books as canon, however, invites us to read individual books in the context of the whole Bible. While we will be mindful of the organic nature of biblical revelation throughout the following study, it will become the object of special focus in chapters ten through twelve.

Question 11: What in Exodus is theologically normative for today? The book of Exodus gives an account of God's working in, to us at least, the far distant past. We live over three thousand years after the events described in the book. Most significantly, the life, death and resurrection of Jesus Christ—the climactic moment in redemptive history—occurred between our time and the exodus generation. As a result, we cannot assume that the theology or the law of Exodus is still relevant for us today. God, the warrior, destroyed the Egyptian army at the Sea. Does God fight through human armies today? The last fifteen chapters of Exodus describe the building of the tabernacle. There is no tabernacle today.

On the other hand, Jesus himself taught in a way that causes us to expect significant continuity between the book of Exodus and today. In the light of Christ's statement that he did not come to "abolish the law of Moses" (Mt 5:17) but that the Law of Moses anticipated his coming (Lk 24:25-27, 44-48), we know that the book of Exodus remains relevant for our theology and practice today. The following chapters will explore the ways in which Exodus continues its importance in our thoughts and actions.

PRINCIPLE 4: REFLECT ON YOUR SITUATION, YOUR SOCIETY'S SITUATION, AND THE GLOBAL SITUATION

The previous question (11) began the transition from trying to understand the meaning of the book to appreciating its continuing significance. While a vast chronological gap exists between our lives today and Moses' time, the book remains relevant. As above, we will here simply raise the questions that will be explored in the chapters to follow.

Question 12: What is my redemptive-historical relationship to the events of Exodus? The story of the Bible is the account of God's pursuit of restoring his broken relationship with human beings. While there is continuity in God's manner of interacting with humanity, there are also changes. The most dramatic moment in the drama of redemption is the death and resurrection of Jesus. Readers of the New Testament understand that these acts instigated tremendous transitions in our relationship with God. Much of the Old Testament was fulfilled by Jesus. We might consider sacrifice as an example. The New Testament teaches that Christ is the ultimate sacrifice, thus rendering animal sacrifice unnecessary (Heb 10:1-18). The Old Testament sacrifices anticipated the sacrifice of Christ. Far from rendering the Old Testament passages irrelevant, Christians read them and apply them in a different way today.[6]

Approaching this subject from a different angle, we must be clear that applying the book of Exodus to our life is not simply a matter of continuing the practices that it affirms and refraining from actions that it prohibits. We have to ask ourselves whether a passage continues to be relevant in precisely the same way or not. Questions to be considered later in the book will be: (1) Is God's rescue of Israel from bondage in Israel a message of hope for enslaved or persecuted people today? (2) Do Christians need to obey the law found in the Book of the Covenant (Ex 19–24)? (3) Do the instructions about the tabernacle continue to be relevant to our understanding of God's presence?

Question 13: What can I learn from Exodus about how to think and act in a way pleasing to God? This question is a continuation of the previous section in that Christian readers of Exodus have to consider the redemptive-historical distance between the events and teaching of the book and their present situation. But other considerations must also be taken into

---

[6]Tremper Longman III, *Immanuel in Our Place* (Phillipsburg, N.J.: P & R, 2001), pp. 75-116.

account as we seek to apply the book to our life. First, we must acknowledge that there are two major types of literature in Exodus, narrative and law. Both of these types of literature raise specific issues concerning the text's continuing relevance. For instance, with narrative, we must always be careful to distinguish the behavior that the text describes from what it approves or disapproves. Recognizing the distinction is often difficult because Hebrew narrative rarely pontificates about the actions of its characters, preferring to show rather than tell. Often we have to judge whether a character's actions are righteous or not by appeal to a didactic part of Scripture. For instance, what about the "lies" of the midwives (Ex 1)? Does Scripture approve of their lying? What implications does this story have for our lives? Does it help us discern situations in which we might withhold the truth or outright lie? Such questions will need to be addressed in the following chapters.

In terms of law, the question becomes a matter of continuity. As we read the New Testament, it appears clear that some laws are no longer relevant. Sacrifice, holy war and the building of the tabernacle are three examples. On the other hand, few would contest the continuing relevance of the commandment not to murder. How can we tell one from the other? And what about a command such as the law to observe the Sabbath? Again, these issues will be addressed in the chapters that follow.

Question 14: How can I keep from imposing my own views on Exodus? Exodus is more than the message of its human author. It is the word of God. Believers will want to hear the word of God. However, the danger of reading our own views into the book is only too present. It would be foolish to think that we can easily transcend our own limited perspective and our own selfish interests as we read the Scripture. Even so, we are not doomed to simply read the book in a way that distorts its message. The following principles are offered to help in this regard:

1. Read prayerfully. Ask God to reveal himself to you in your reading of his word and to preserve you from simply imposing your own ideas on the text. Prayer is not magic, and God does not promise to lead us

to an inerrant interpretation of his word. Even so, prayer puts us in the appropriate attitude of submission to God.

2. Recognize the problem. Being aware that we can read our own ideas into the text is an important step to avoiding doing so. Question your interpretations. Ask why you are interpreting it in the way you are.

3. Read the interpretations of others. If you are reading this book, you obviously are willing to do so. Commentaries are particularly helpful in this regard. For that reason I have included a commentary guide to the book of Exodus at the end of this book (appendix 2).

SUMMARY OF THE INTERPRETIVE QUESTIONS

1. What kind of book is Exodus?

2. How did ancient Hebrews tell stories?

3. Was Exodus written at one time by a single person?

4. What can we learn about Exodus from comparable ancient Near Eastern literature?

5. When was Exodus written?

6. What does Exodus tell us about the past?

7. Does our knowledge of the ancient Near East help us understand Exodus?

8. How does Exodus describe God?

9. How does Exodus describe God's relationship to his people?

10. How does Exodus fit into the whole of Scripture?

11. What in Exodus is theologically normative for today?

12. What is my redemptive-historical relationship to the events of Exodus?

13. What can I learn from Exodus about how to think and act in a way pleasing to God?

14. How can I keep from imposing my views on Exodus?

FOR FURTHER READING

Fee, Gordon, and Douglas Stuart. *How to Read the Bible for All Its Worth.* 3rd ed. Grand Rapids: Zondervan, 2003.

Firth, David, and Jamie A. Grant, eds. *Words and the Word: Explorations in Biblical Interpretation and Literary Theory.* Downers Grove, Ill.: InterVarsity Press, 2008.

Klein, William W., Craig L. Blomberg and Robert L. Hubbard Jr. *Introduction to Biblical Interpretation.* 2nd ed. Nashville: Thomas Nelson, 2004.

Longman, Tremper, III. *How to Read Genesis.* Downers Grove, Ill.: InterVarsity Press, 2005.

―――. *Reading the Bible with Heart and Mind.* Colorado Springs, Colo.: NavPress, 1997.

PART

2

READING EXODUS
AS LITERATURE

■   ■   ■

TWO

THE SHAPE OF
THE BOOK OF EXODUS

We begin our study of the book of Exodus by exploring its literary features, in particular its genre, outline and style. Biblical authors were attentive to how they delivered their message as well as its content. To fully appreciate the book we have to examine the author's strategy of presentation. The following chapter focuses on the final form of the book of Exodus and does not consider questions concerning how the book achieved its present condition. Appendix one in the back of the book raises issues concerning the history of the book's composition. While not denying the importance of the history of the book's composition, it is also important to analyze the book's final form as the one that the church has recognized as authoritative for the faith and practice of Christians.

THE GENRE OF EXODUS
Authors do not often create whole new forms; they write in a way that conforms to literary types that are already known to the audience. Otherwise the reader wouldn't know how to interpret the words on the page. In this way literary genres are like language. Both are codes that are

shared by writer and reader. If an author used a previously unknown word, or used a word in a totally new way without explanation, then the reader would have no idea what it meant. In the same way, if the author created a whole new way of writing, the reader would not know how to read the work. Genres signal a reader how to take the words on the page; they trigger a reading strategy. Is a work a piece of fiction or history? Is it a parable or an adventure story? A misunderstanding or misconstrual of a book's genre will distort its message.

What kind of book is Exodus? Is it a legend, a history book, a parable, a law book, or something else?

The most natural response to reading the beginning of Exodus is to understand it as talking about past events, in other words the book appears to be a book of history. True, some scholars (the minimalists, see in chapter 5) argue that the book is a fictionalized history, but even they admit that the author intends readers to take the book as a history. They believe that a group of immigrants into Palestine in the Persian or Hellenistic period are laying divine claim to the land by creating the impression that God had given that land to their ancestors.

My point is that there is fairly universal understanding that the book of Exodus is in some shape or form a work of history. The disagreement concerns whether the history is true or not. That question will be addressed in chapters five and six.

It would be misleading, however, to leave the discussion of genre simply by calling the book a work of history. The history genre is united by concern to narrate actual events that happened in space and time, but a moment's reflection reminds us that the account of history is not the same as the events themselves. History writing is a verbal representation of those events much like a portrait painting is a representation of a person.[1] Different painters might render a portrait of the same individual, and while they all might be said to be true to their subject, they likely would all be different depending on such factors as the painter's style, the aspects of the physical appearance of the subject

---

[1]See V. P. Long, *The Art of Biblical History* (Grand Rapids: Zondervan, 1994), pp. 63-68.

that they attended to, the mood that they associated with the person, and so forth.

Representing past events in history writing involves selection and interpretation. Writers cannot report every detail of an event, but must be selective, including only what is important to the message they are communicating. The presentation of a historical event is shaped by the interpretive lens that the writer adopts.

We must then ask what is the purpose of the book of Exodus. What is the author trying to communicate? The book, as we mentioned above, is about the founding of Israel as a nation. It explains how Israel was freed from Egyptian bondage and given a law that serves as its constitution and also a communal place of worship. This particular account of these events is furthermore intent on demonstrating that all of these were the result of God's gift, an act of divine grace. Thus, the events chosen and the interpretive lens through which they are narrated serves the purpose of showing God's hands in the events that lead to the formation of Israel as a nation. Such an understanding of the overall genre will affect the form of the outline of the book which we will give in the next section.

In light of our recognition of the intent of the writer, we can further specify Exodus' genre. There are different types of history with different emphases: e.g., military history, legal history, economic history or literary history. I like to describe Exodus (and other similar books in the Bible) as theological history focusing on God's relationship with Israel and involving God's self-disclosure. This does not mean that there are not accounts of wars, politics and economics, but they are in service of a theological message.

Finally, though I believe it right to call Exodus as a whole theological history, this book incorporates other genres of literature as well. Most notably, Exodus contains a lengthy section of law. Law as genre will be examined in chapter 8, but here notice how it is integrated into the flow of history as presented in the book. Another significant genre in the book is song, which has the form of poetry (Ex 15). While space does not allow us to discuss the conventions of Hebrew poetry, the interested reader can consult the appropriate section in my previous books in this series.[2]

THE OUTLINE OF THE BOOK OF EXODUS

Having an outline of a book in mind can help the reader navigate the book as a whole. Books can be structured in more than one way. Some scholars,[3] for instance, provide an outline of Exodus based on location:

I. *Israel in Egypt (1:1–13:16)*
II. *Israel in the Wilderness (13:17–18:27)*
III. *Israel in Sinai (19:1–40:38)*

This book will follow a slightly different outline based on the contents and three major themes of the book: deliverance, law and presence.

I. *God Saves Israel from Egyptian Bondage (1–18)*
II. *God Gives Israel His Law (19–24)*
III. *God Commands Israel to Build the Tabernacle (25–40)*

Notice too how this outline emphasizes a characteristic of the book mentioned above: God's initiative. God is the one who delivers Israel, gives them the law that defines them as a nation, and instructs them concerning the building of the tabernacle where he will make his presence known among them. Chapters seven through nine will follow this outline in the exposition of the book's content.

THE STYLE OF EXODUS

Under genre we noted that the book is theological history interspersed with law. Indeed, on occasion law and narrative interpenetrate each other. A good example of this is Exodus 12, where the event of the Passover is also a mandate for future observance of the annual festival.

Theological history is given in a narrative format, and the observant

---

[2]Tremper Longman III, *How to Read Psalms* (Downers Grove, Ill.: InterVarsity Press, 1987), pp. 89-94; idem., *How to Read Proverbs* (Downers Grove, Ill.: InterVarsity Press, 2002), pp. 37-46.

[3]For instance, J. I. Durham, *Exodus* (Waco, Tex.: Word, 1987).

reader will be alert to the conventions of Hebrew narrative style, including plot, characterization and setting. As Robert Alter, the doyen of modern literary study of the Bible, says, "It is important to keep in mind the peculiarity of the Hebrew mode of presentation because that will help us learn where to look for its revelations of meaning."[4] Of course, it is important to interpret any individual passage in the book in the light of the overarching plot. The plot of the story is presented by a narrator. As is typical in Hebrew narrative, the story is told by an anonymous, third-person, omniscient narrator. If Moses is the (an) author, he does not speak from a first-person perspective. The book (and the Pentateuch) does not name an author anyway (see appendix 1). The use of third-person, omniscient narrative gives the impression that the story is being told by none other than God.

It is the narrator who gives us insight into the lives of the characters. Of course, behind the narrator lies the author, but however we characterize it the point is that we know only what we are told. It is interesting, for instance (and a matter of comment later), that the narrator never refers to the Pharaoh by name. As we notice this, we should ask why? How does that affect our attitude toward this character?

As we study the book of Exodus we should also pay attention to two other features that are considered important by students of Hebrew narrative style. First, special attention should be paid to speech. Often the plot is furthered by speech rather than description of the event. Indeed, a major focus of interest is in the reactions of characters to events as revealed by their speech. Notice, for instance, the brief section that reports the interaction between the Pharaoh and the Hebrew midwives in Exodus 1:15-19. The dialogue outstrips the narrative. Pharaoh's speech marks him as callous and blundering, while the midwives come across as intelligent and brave.

The second important feature of Hebrew narrative to point out is its reticence. The narrator rarely gives motivations. When the motivations are expressed in the text, they are usually by the characters themselves

---

[4]Robert Alter, *The Art of Biblical Narrative* (New York: Basic Books, 1981), p. 64.

and the readers are left to wonder whether the characters are speaking the truth. To illustrate this we turn to the episode of the Golden Calf. Moses comes down from the mountain where he has received the law, only to encounter Israel under Aaron's leadership worshiping an idol in the form of a calf. The narrator does not tell us why Aaron allowed it, but instead reports his answer to Moses' question. "You know yourself how evil these people are. They said to me, 'Make us some gods who will lead us. We don't know what happened to this fellow Moses, who brought us here from the land of Egypt.' So I told them, 'Whoever has gold jewelry, take it off.' When they brought it to me, I simply threw it into the fire—and out came this calf!" (Ex 32:22-24). The narrator does not affirm or deny this self-assessment. The reader has to reflect on it to determine whether it is trustworthy. The idea that the calf popped out of the fire after the jewelry was thrown in is so unbelievable, though, as to throw a gigantic question mark over his response.

As a matter of fact, the narrator's reticence to express motives as well as physical description causes the reader to enter more deeply into the story. It raises questions that get us to read more closely.

These general features of Hebrew narrative style shape our reception of the story. In later chapters we will from time to time draw attention back to these conventions as well as note more detailed points of Hebrew style in both narrative and law.

PRINCIPLES FOR READING

1. Determine what the text indicates concerning its history of composition. How did Exodus reach its final form (see appendix 1)?

2. No matter what conclusion is reached in answer to the first point, the interpreter should treat the final form of the text as a whole.

3. Identify the genre of the book.

4. Determine the outline of the book.

5. Be sensitive to the literary style of the book.

FOR FURTHER READING

Alter, Robert. *The Art of Biblical Narrative.* New York: Basic Books, 1981.

Baroody, W. G., and W. F. Gentrup. "Exodus, Leviticus, Numbers, and Deuteronomy," pp. 121-36. In *The Complete Literary Guide to the Bible,* edited by Leland Ryken and Tremper Longman III. Grand Rapids: Zondervan, 1993.

Berlin, Adele. *Poetics and Interpretation of Biblical Narrative.* Sheffield: Almond, 1983.

Fokkelman, J. P. "Exodus," pp. 56-65. In *The Literary Guide to the Bible,* edited by R. Alter and F. Kermode. Cambridge, Mass.: Harvard University Press, 1987.

Longman, Tremper, III. *A Literary Approach to Biblical Interpretation.* Grand Rapids: Zondervan, 1987.

Sternberg, Meir. *The Poetics of Biblical Narrative.* Bloomington: Indiana University Press, 1985.

THREE

THE NARRATIVE STRUCTURE
OF EXODUS

Presence, Covenant and Servitude

The book of Exodus is a theological history. That is, it narrates what actually happened in the past, but does so in a way that presents a compelling picture of God. This picture of God, though, is not abstract. Rather, God is always described in relationship with his people. The author of Exodus is more than a theologian or a historian, he is a master storyteller utilizing the literary conventions (see chapter 1, pp. 15-19) of his day to present a stirring narrative of God's interaction with his people.

Exodus is not a collection of isolated traditions that have only a loose connection with each other. One might get that impression from the fact that the book is a mixture of story, poetry, liturgy and law. A number of important themes provide an overarching narrative structure (plot) to the book. Discerning the narrative structure is instrumental to the development of a reading strategy of the book of Exodus.

As implied in the above paragraph, it is my belief that there is more than one theme that can help us understand the narrative structure of the book. Even so, it may be possible to highlight one that is most important in that it is the most explicit and pervasive theme of the book. That theme is, simply stated, the presence of God. With that in mind, we will begin this chapter with an exposition of the plot that shows the move from the absence to the presence of God among the community of Israel.

Related to this theme is the theme of the covenant. Indeed, the covenant is not so much a second theme as it is the metaphorical vehicle that God uses to explain the nature of his relationship with Israel. In short, the covenant is the reason why God chooses to be present with Israel. However, by treating it separately we can more effectively demonstrate its importance to the book.

Yet a third theme of the book has to do with bondage. In the beginning Israel is in bondage to Egypt; at the end of the book, they are still in bondage, but to Yahweh, a benevolent slave master. We will conclude the chapter with an exposition of the theme of servitude.

FROM ABSENCE TO PRESENCE

When the book of Genesis ended, the family of God had moved to Egypt from the Promised Land of Canaan. Jacob, his sons, and the rest of the family went to Egypt to survive a famine, and God allowed them to prosper there. Joseph had providentially risen from slave to important leader in the country, having engineered Egypt's own survival of the devastating famine. For Joseph's sake, the Egyptian Pharaoh settled them in Goshen, a land where they could pursue their occupation as those who raised livestock.

Heavenly silence: Israel in bondage. Some centuries have passed by the time the action of Exodus begins, so the book reminds the reader of the family's earlier move to Egypt (Ex 1:1-5). Interestingly God is not mentioned until the end of the first chapter of Exodus. The first fourteen verses describe how Israel has grown so much in population that they constitute a threat to Egypt, compelling Pharaoh to command the enslavement of Israel and the killing of their male children.

It is notable that no theological reason is given for this downturn in the fate of Israel. Unlike many other places in Scripture, Israel's suffering is not grounded in their sin. Indeed, no explanation is given. Nonetheless, we should be hesitant to read too much into this gap. While it might be tempting to think that Israel somehow wandered from their allegiance to the true God, in the absence of any biblical statement to that effect, we must leave the cause open. The book of Job, among other texts, will caution against the easy equation between sin and suffering. Furthermore, notice that God does not require Israel to repent before he delivers them from their bondage.

Even so, there is a noticeable lack of mention of God when the book opens, and when God is first mentioned, he is linked with the faithful Israelite midwives who fear him and not with the entire community (Ex 1:15-22). Even though God was good to the midwives, the Israelites were still slaves and their baby boys were presumably still being murdered, no matter how many were saved by the midwives' courageous act.

Even in the dramatic story of Moses' birth (Ex 2:1-10), God is strangely absent, at least explicitly. Of course Moses not only survived but, ironically, was raised in Pharaoh's household with his own mother as a wet nurse. Surely the text means for us to see God's providential hand behind these events. Even so, we must acknowledge that God is not explicit in the text.

So too in the episode when Moses kills the Egyptian who brutalized an Israelite worker (Ex 2:11-24). Where is God during this event? Moses was forced to flee and settle with the Midianites in the wilderness.

God makes his presence known to Moses. Up to this point God seems strangely absent from his people. However, the turning point comes at the end of the second chapter:

> Years passed, and the king of Egypt died. But the Israelites continued to groan under their burden of slavery. They cried out for help, and their cry rose up to God. God heard their groaning, and he remembered his covenant promise to Abraham, Isaac, and Jacob. He looked down on the people of Israel and knew it was time to act. (Ex 2:23-25)

The Israelites cried for help. While in Judges the Israelites' cry represented their repentance from their sin, explicitly stated in the text, this cry arises not as a cry of repentance but as a cry of pain. Note that their "cry rose to God." He was not in their midst, but at a distance. Thus, "he looked down on the people of Israel." Their cry stirred him on their behalf. He would initiate actions that would lead to an intimate involvement with his people. Later we will consider the covenantal aspect of his action.

Rather than coming to Israel in Egypt directly, God meets Moses in the wilderness, at Mount Sinai. He makes his presence known to this future human deliverer of Israel before he makes it known to the people in Egypt. He reveals himself at this time and place in the form of a bush that burns but is not consumed (chap. 3). As we will observe as we move on in the story, God often makes his presence known in the form of fire and smoke. Fire destroys and grants warmth and life. Fire compels attention, but also shrouds (along with smoke) what stands behind it. The fire and smoke are not God, but they represent his presence.

At this critical moment, God reveals himself to Moses outside of Egypt where his people presently live, and he sends Moses as his messenger to Israel in Egypt. Moses is a mediator of divine presence and power (God promises Moses that he will be with him in Ex 3:12), but God does not reveal himself to the people as he did to Moses until they prepare to leave Egypt. It is not as if he does not have a presence or power there. He is after all omnipresent, but he is not making his presence explicit to the people of Israel in the way that he is now doing to Moses. Rather God sends Moses with a message to the people and to Pharaoh. God wants Moses to bring Israel to Mount Sinai where he can meet with them, and there he will reveal his presence to them with power.

Moses, at first reluctant and with the aid of his brother Aaron, then journeys to Egypt to fulfill the mission that God has given him. As mentioned, God does not at this time make his presence known to the Israelites in the same way that he did to Moses at Mount Sinai. He does not speak to the people, except through Moses and Aaron. He does not even appear in the form of fire and smoke. Of course, he does make his presence known to them through the mighty works of power he performs in the plagues that he brought against Egypt. Indeed, it may be that God's presence is subtly indicated by the rods of Moses and Aaron. These are the rods that they threw to the ground and which turned into serpents in the first sign in Pharaoh's court. These are the rods that they raised or manipulated in some way to initiate many of the plagues (Ex 4:17; 7:9-10, 19, etc.). Climactically, Moses raised his rod and the Re(e)d Sea split in two (Ex 14:16). Even after the crossing of the Sea and before coming to Mount Sinai, Moses' rod likely indicated God's presence when he raised it to victory against the Amalekites in Exodus 17.

Interestingly, once Israel leaves Egypt we hear that a pillar of cloud leads them by the day and a pillar of fire at night (Ex 13:20-22), and that Yahweh "went ahead of them." The pillar of cloud also assumed a defensive position between the Egyptian army and the Israelite camp as the Egyptians prepared to attack them at the Re(e)d Sea. Interestingly though, rather than simply saying that it was Yahweh who was leading them it names "the angel of God" (Ex 14:19-20) as the one who was leading them at this time. Even so, it is likely that this angel was the "concrete manifestation of God's presence with his people."[1]

God's revelation to the assembly at Mount Sinai. While acknowledging God's role in the departure from Egypt and at the Re(e)d Sea, in another important sense Israel journeyed into the wilderness to go to Mount Sinai where they would meet God and experience his presence in a new and more profound way. Indeed, the Israelites remain at Sinai through the rest of the book of Exodus (until Num 10:10). Exodus 19 records the meeting of God and the Israelites. Here God makes his presence known to the whole community of Israel in a manner analogous to Moses meeting God at the burning bush. Of course a burning bush would not suffice for the entire Israelite community. Even so, God similarly makes his presence known by means of fire and smoke, though in a larger and more public way. According to Exodus 19:18, "All of Mount Sinai was covered with smoke because the Lord had descended on it in the form of fire. The smoke billowed into the sky like smoke from a

---

[1]Peter Enns, *Exodus* (Grand Rapids: Zondervan, 2000), p. 275.

brick kiln, and the whole mountain shook violently." Though Moses continued to act as a mediator between God and the people, God had clearly made his presence known to his people in a new and dramatic way. The last section of the book of Exodus tells the story of the means by which God communicated with Israel that his presence would continue to abide with them.

The tabernacle. Later chapters (see chapters 4, 9, 12) will describe the tabernacle in greater detail. For the purpose of following the narrative theme of presence, we will simply point out that the main purpose of this lengthy and climactic section of Exodus (essentially Ex 25–40) is to show how God will now make his presence a permanent part of the community of Israel. The tabernacle is God's home on earth, the place where he dwells in the midst of his people. While the entirety of the tabernacle and its furniture indicate that God is present, the Ark of the Covenant in particular is the most potent symbol of God's presence (see p. 135).

Between command and fulfillment of the instructions to build the tabernacle, the Israelites threaten the relationship between themselves and God by worshiping the Golden Calf. When Moses descends from the top of the mountain with the two tablets of the law, he throws them down and breaks them, signifying the breaking of the relationship between God and Israel.

Whether God will dwell with his people or even let them survive becomes a real question in the aftermath of the people's rebellion. God tells Moses to continue to lead the people but that "I will not travel among you, for you are a stubborn and rebellious people. If I did, I would surely destroy you along the way" (Ex 33:3). God's Tent of Meeting was then placed outside the camp where God would make his presence known to Israel in the form of a cloud. Moses would meet God there and "the LORD would speak to Moses face to face, as one speaks to a friend" (Ex 33:11).

In response to Moses' intercession, God decides to go with the people. He further gives Moses an unprecedented experience of the divine glory. This momentous event is described as Moses standing in a cleft of a rock and then seeing God as he passed by. It is unprecedented but not a total exposure to the presence of God (Ex 33:23, "I will remove my hand and let you see me from behind. But my face will not be seen"). Moses' special experience of God's presence was literally etched in his face, necessitating his wearing a veil when he was with the people (Ex 34:29-34).

With the crisis over, since God was now determined to go with the people, the tabernacle is built. The climax of the book of Exodus is the final passage that describes the cloud filling the completed structure (Ex 40:34-35). The text anticipates the books that follow as it describes how the cloud, symbolizing God's presence, will lift up and guide the Israelites through the wilderness by day, and at night it will be fiery (again combining smoke and fire) to guide them in the darkness.

COVENANT: I WILL BE YOUR GOD AND
YOU WILL BE MY PEOPLE

Extensive descriptions and expositions of the covenant may be found elsewhere.[2] The covenant is a legal metaphor defining the nature of the relationship between two parties. Recent studies have more precisely pinpointed the nature of the covenant as a particular type of legal relationship, a vassal treaty.[3] In such a treaty, a great nation enters into a relationship with a less powerful nation. In such treaties, one can typically find a rehearsal of the relationship between the two parties (the historical review), laws that the sovereign king imposes on the vassal king, rewards and punishments that follow on the keeping or breaking of the law, and a list of those who witness the making of the treaty. In some places in Scripture where God establishes or renews a covenant with his people these elements may be clearly seen in their entirety

---

[2]A sample list includes W. J. Dumbrell, *Covenant and Creation* (Carlisle, U.K.: Paternoster, 1984); T. E. McComiskey, *The Covenants of Promise: A Theology of the Old Testament* (Grand Rapids: Baker, 1985); O. P. Robertson, *The Christ of the Covenants* (Philippsburg, N.J.: P & R, 1980); J. Niehaus, *God at Sinai* (Grand Rapids: Zondervan, 1995).

[3]Note for instance, M. G. Kline, *Treaty of the Great King* (Grand Rapids: Eerdmans, 1963); D. J. McCarthy, *Old Testament Covenant: A Survey of Current Opinions*, 2nd ed. (Rome: Pontifical Biblical Institute, 1978).

(Deut; Josh 24; 1 Sam 12, for instance). That is not clearly the case in Exodus. Even so, the covenant plays a major role in the book, which is not surprising since at the heart of the book God enters into a covenant with his people (Ex 19–24). At this point, we are not interested in the full development of this theme. Rather we want to alert the reader to the role that covenant plays in the development of the absence of divine presence theme articulated above.

When the book of Exodus opens, we hear that Israel has multiplied greatly (Ex 1:6-10). Israel's expanded population brings to mind the Abrahamic covenant with its divine promises to the patriarch: "I will make you into a great nation. I will bless you and make you famous, and you will be a blessing to others. I will bless those who bless you and curse those who treat you with contempt. All the families of the earth will be blessed through you" (Gen 12:2-3). As these covenant promises are treated in the patriarchal narratives, it becomes very clear that a large population is essential to its fulfillment. When, for instance, God comes and reassures Abraham of his intention to fulfill the promises, he renews the covenant and proclaims: "Look up into the sky and count the stars if you can. That's how many descendants you will have!" (Gen 15:5). Thus, the indication that Israel has grown so much hints that the conditions for the fulfillment of the covenant are at hand.

Indeed, in the covenant renewal in Genesis 15, God had anticipated the conditions that existed in Exodus 1: "You can be sure that your descendants will be strangers in a foreign land, where they will be oppressed as slaves for 400 years. But I will punish that nation that enslaves them, and in the end they will come away with great wealth" (Gen 15:13-14). At the opening of Exodus, Israel is enslaved in a foreign land. The next step is rescue!

We should not be surprised, then, that the narrator cites the Abrahamic covenant as the motivating force behind God's intention to release his people from their slavery: "God heard their groaning, and he remembered his covenant promise to Abraham, Isaac, and Jacob. He looked down on the people of Israel and knew it was time to act" (Ex 2:24-25; see also Ex 3:7-8, 16-22; 13:5, 11). Thus the story of the exodus from Egypt (Ex 1–18) has at its heart the Abrahamic covenant where God promised to be Israel's God and that Israel would be God's people. The purpose of the exodus, covenantally understood, was to take God's people back to the Promised Land and establish them as a "great nation" who enjoyed a special relationship with God.

The next section of the book narrates a new covenantal relationship with Israel. This covenant mediated by Moses did not replace the earlier covenant with Abraham. It now establishes and maintains a relationship between God and Israel, now that the latter is constituted a nation. In the words of P. Williamson, "the Sinaitic covenant spells out the type of nation that Yahweh intends Israel to be."[4]

This nation is to be God's own "special treasure" (Ex 19:5), implying an intimate relationship. But, of course, there are obligations as well as privileges associated with the covenant. After all, they were to be a blessing to the nations (also in fulfillment of the Abrahamic covenant). Exodus expresses this outward-looking mission by saying that Israel was to be a "kingdom of priests, my holy nation" (Ex 19:6). The law, which constitutes the bulk of Exodus 19–24, is thus a covenantal law, showing them how to be holy. No wonder that Moses offers sacrifices and Israel a banquet to seal the covenantal relationship (Ex 24). That the blood is sprinkled on both the altar and the people shows the two-sided nature of the covenant.

God then makes his presence known, as we have seen above, in a more direct manner when the covenant is being ratified at Mount Sinai. We have already seen that this intimate relationship and God's intention to make his presence remain with Israel are threatened by their breaking the covenant by their worship of the Golden Calf. Moses' breaking the tablets of the law forcibly and vividly demonstrates how Israel's breaking of the law leads to a breaking of the relationship with God.

Moses, however, intercedes on their behalf and God reestablishes his

---

[4]P. Williamson, "Covenant," in *Dictionary of the Old Testament: Pentateuch*, ed. T. Desmond Alexander and David W. Baker (Downers Grove, Ill.: InterVarsity Press, 2003), p. 150. The whole article is instructive concerning the covenant in the Pentateuch (pp. 139-55).

relationship with them. Thus, the tabernacle, representing God's presence, can be built. The role of the Sabbath in the narration of the tabernacle may well point to the covenantal nature of that building. The covenant, after all, is the sign of the Mosaic covenant (Ex 32:13), and instructions concerning the Sabbath conclude the instructions to build the tabernacle (Ex 31:12-18) and open the account of its actual construction (Ex 35:1-3).[5] Perhaps even more obvious for the relationship between the tabernacle and the covenant is the fact that the focus of attention in the former is on the Ark, the repository of the Ten Commandments, and often called the Ark of the Covenant (or its synonym, Testimony, see Ex 25:22).

In summary, the covenant is of major importance to the book of Exodus and is related closely to the first theme, the presence of God. We have seen that God moves toward enslaved Israel on the basis of the Abrahamic covenant, and then after he frees them from their bondage, he establishes a new covenant with them that builds on the earlier patriarchal covenant. This new covenant binds Israel to their God. It demands from Israel obedience to the laws presented in that covenant in order to maintain their special relationship with God. This leads to the third and final theme that we will explore in this chapter: From bondage to Egypt to bondage to Yahweh.

FROM BONDAGE TO EGYPT TO BONDAGE TO YAHWEH

Our final theme is bondage, or servitude. This theme interacts with the other themes of the book, but it is illuminating to consider it on its own. We can be brief in our outline of this theme now that we have examined presence and covenant as important ideas in the book.

When the book opens, Israel is in bondage to Pharaoh and he is an oppressive figure. He has enslaved the Israelites and put them to work on the building of the two cites of Pithom and Rameses (Ex 1:11). He fears their growing numbers, so he orders the execution of male children. Pharaoh is the epitome of a malign dictator. He is powerful and

---

[5]See Williamson, "Covenant," pp. 151-52, citing Dumbrell, *Covenant and Creation*.

cruel and seemingly beyond challenge.

God rescues Israel from bondage to this human king. But does he move them from bondage to freedom? Yes, if that freedom is conceived as freedom from Egypt, but their new condition is not that of autonomous individuals. They have been freed from service to Egypt and brought into the service of God.[6]

The covenant, as we have seen above, defines and maintains the relationship between God, the heavenly king, and his vassal people Israel. The Book of the Covenant (Ex 19–24) presents the laws of the heavenly king to his people. They must obey them. Further, they are called into the service of their God.

This last point brings us to an interesting change of the use within the book of Exodus of the Hebrew word *aboda*. The basic meaning of this word in English is something like "work." At the beginning of the book, the word is used to describe the compelled labor of the Israelites to Egypt. Indeed, it could be understood as "slave labor" in Exodus 1:14; 2:23; 5:9, 11; 6:6, 9. The same word though is also used for the labor that God requires in Exodus 12:25-26; 13:5; 27:19; 30:16; 35:24; 36:1, 3, 5; 39:32, 42. Thus, though in a real sense it is appropriate to speak of the exodus as a move from bondage to freedom, where freedom means from a cruel oppression, it is also true that the exodus is more carefully described as a movement from one master to another. The new master has his subjects' best interests in mind. True freedom is found in service to the Lord. Fretheim states this theme well when he says, "the book of Exodus moves from slavery to worship, from Israel's bondage to Pharaoh to its bonding to Yahweh. More particularly, the book moves from enforced construction of the buildings for Pharaoh to the glad and obedient offering of the people for a building for the worship of God."[7]

Presence, covenant and bondage/service are three central themes in the book of Exodus. Of course, our analysis of these themes does not exhaust the literary and theological richness of the book, but it gives the

---

[6]As my editor and friend Dan Reid likes to put it, it is a move from tedium to Te Deum. I want to thank Dan for alerting me to the presence of this theme in the book of Exodus.
[7]Terence E. Fretheim, *Exodus* (Louisville: John Knox, 1991), p. 1.

reader a sense of the thematic coherence of the book and helps us develop a strategy to read the book.

QUESTIONS FOR DISCUSSION

1. If God is omnipresent (that is, he is everywhere: see Psalm 139), how can we say that he is absent from Israel at the beginning of the chapter? What does God's absence mean?

2. Why would God use a political and legal term like the covenant as one of the main metaphors describing his relationship with his people?

3. What are some other metaphors that Exodus uses to describe the relationship between God and his people? What are other metaphors used in other places in the Bible?

4. The three themes studied in the chapter are just three of the most prominent. There are others. Can you name and describe them?

FOR FURTHER READING

Baroody, W. G., and W. F. Gentrup, "Exodus, Leviticus, Numbers, and Deuteronomy," pp. 95-107. In *A Complete Literary Guide to the Bible,* ed. Leland Ryken and Tremper Longman III, Grand Rapids: Zondervan, 1993.

Fokkelman, J. P. "Exodus," pp. 56-65. In *The Literary Guide to the Bible,* R. Alter and F. Kermode. Cambridge, Mass.: Harvard University Press, 1987.

Fretheim, Terence E. *Exodus*. Interpretation. Louisville: John Knox, 1991.

Mann, T. W. *Divine Presence and Guidance in Israelite Traditions: The Typology of Exaltation*. Baltimore: Johns Hopkins University Press, 1977.

Sarna, N. M. *Exploring Exodus: The Origins of Biblical Israel*. New York: Schocken, 1996.

Williamson, P. "Covenant," pp. 139-55. In *Dictionary of the Old Testament: Pentateuch,* ed. T. D. Alexander and D. W. Baker. Downers Grove, Ill.: InterVarsity Press, 2003.

P A R T

3

READING EXODUS AS HISTORY

IN ITS HISTORICAL CONTEXT

■   ■   ■

In our exploration of the genre of Exodus (chapter 2), we concluded that the book was theological history and that the modifier "theological" did not diminish the noun "history." In other words, the author(s) of Exodus want readers to understand the narrative as actual space and time events. Of course, the fact that authors want their readers to take their narrative as historical does not make it true. The present section will explore the historicity of the Exodus account. It will also situate the book in its ancient Near Eastern setting. Finally, we ask whether the issue matters. Does it matter if the Exodus actually took place?

FOUR

BIRTH LEGENDS, HAMMURABI
AND PORTABLE SHRINES

The Ancient Near Eastern Background of Exodus

The Bible was not written in a cultural vacuum. If one takes the biblical account of Moses' life seriously, he was likely educated in an Egyptian context since he was raised in the household of Pharaoh. The people of Israel themselves were probably not formally educated, but certainly ideas about life and religion percolated in families and in the community. As the Israelites worked on the store cities (Ex 1:11), they would have noted the sculptures and paintings of Egyptian history and gods. The Egyptians would have surely made many of their laws known to them. Eventually Moses would lead them toward the Promised Land, inhabited by the Canaanites who had their own distinctive religion and culture. Again, as an educated man, Moses would have knowledge of Canaanite culture, which was closer to Mesopotamian ideas than Egyptian.

Reflecting on Israel's cultural environment reminds us that the book of Exodus is best understood with knowledge of ancient Near Eastern customs, literature and history. Our knowledge of the cultural and literary background to the Bible has greatly increased since the nineteenth century when the modern period of archaeological exploration of the Middle East began to recover the languages and literature of these societies. The following chapter will demonstrate how the knowledge of ancient Near Eastern materials can aid us in understanding the book of Exodus. The book's basic theological message can certainly be understood without reference to these materials, but such knowledge can deepen our appreciation, make the story more vivid, and give us a better idea about how it was heard in its original setting.

Unfortunately, space does not allow us to be exhaustive but only illustrative in our survey of the ancient Near Eastern background in this chapter. Three topics have been chosen for examination: the story of the birth of Moses, the law and the shape of the tabernacle. In addition, we have on occasion pointed to the ancient Near Eastern background of specific texts in the exposition of the book found in chapters seven through nine.

THE BIRTH OF MOSES AND THE BIRTH OF SARGON
The story of Moses' birth (Ex 2:1-10) is well known. Moses' mother, Jochebed (Ex 6:20), gave birth to a baby boy in the dark shadow of the Egyptian decree to kill all Israelite boys. The midwives were of the habit of showing up late to the births of children over whose death they were to preside according to the decree of Pharaoh, giving Jochebed time to act. She hid him for three months, but when he grew too big to hide any longer, she constructed a "papyrus basket" for him and coated it with tar and pitch. She placed the baby in the basket and placed it on the Nile. It is no coincidence that the word for "basket" here is *tebah*, the word used otherwise only for Noah's ark in Genesis 6–9. Though of drastically different size, both refer to objects that float on water and bear passengers. The use in the Exodus passage is surely to call on the reader to think of Noah's ark. Both vessels carry their occupants to safety; they are instruments of God's gracious salvation.

Besides the background in Genesis, we turn to an interesting ancient Near Eastern background in an Akkadian text called the Sargon Birth

Legend.[1] The subject of the story is Sargon the Great (ca. 2334–2279 B.C.), though it was written during the reign of a later Assyrian king also with the name Sargon (late eighth century B.C.). The text is autobiographical, so the story is told from Sargon's perspective as an adult.[2] By this time, he had assumed the kingship of Agade (the Akkadian empire) from humble beginnings. The purpose of his birth story was to show that, though he came from nowhere, he really had a noble birth.

His mother was a high priestess. The assumption of the text is that the high priestess should not have children (except perhaps by the king). Thus, like Moses' mother she could not keep her child. For that reason, Sargon says, "she placed me in a reed basket, she sealed my hatch with pitch" (compare Ex 2:3) and placed him on the river. The basket floated down the river until an irrigation worker, Aqqi, spotted it. He raised baby Sargon who went on to become king.

The similarities of the birth stories are notable. So much so that some suspect that the Moses story is simply an adaptation of the Sargon story and that both are really simply folklore providing answers to the question: Where did these "nobodies" come from before they grew so important?

We must, however, first notice an interesting contrast between the two stories. Sargon's origins are noble, though he was raised in humble circumstances. Moses, on the other hand, was born to a slave family, but the basket brought him to a noble family. He did not go on to become king of a great nation, but the founding leader of a humble people.

Still the hypothesis that there is any direct connection between these two stories is unnecessary. Due to problems of dating both texts, it would be hard to insist that one came before the other, though our own views of the dating of Exodus and the Sargon text would actually indicate that the former came before the latter. Even so, the similarity is better explained by common custom rather than literary borrowing.

---

[1]For a convenient translation, see B. R. Foster's in *Context of Scripture*, vol. 1, ed. W. W. Hallo and K. Lawson Younger (Leiden: Brill, 1997), p. 461.

[2]Tremper Longman III, *Fictional Akkadian Autobiography* (Winona Lake, Ind.: Eisenbrauns, 1991), pp. 53-60.

That is, Sargon and Moses' mothers may well be acting according to the custom of the day. Granted the custom is not explained in so many words, but it makes sense of the action. Placing a child in a basket on a river seems like strange behavior to us today, but it was likely the customary act of women who could not keep children but did not want to dispose of them (such children were left exposed to the elements in antiquity). In essence, through their actions they commit their children into the care of their gods. Their gods would rescue their children. In Jochebed's case, Moses not only survived, she was allowed to become the wet nurse (Ex 2:7-10)!

The significance of reading the account of Moses' birth on the background of the Sargon Birth Legend is that it gives us additional insight into the motivations of his mother's actions. She was putting her trust in God who came through for her. Moses not only survived but she was allowed to raise him. The Pharaoh's desire to thwart Israel through his decree to kill the baby boys was itself thwarted. The future savior of Israel was raised under his very roof.

MOSES' LAW AND THE CODE OF HAMMURABI

God gave Israel the law through Moses on Mount Sinai. At the foundation of the law stands the Ten Commandments written on two stone tablets. Flowing from the Ten Commandments are a number of laws that are specific applications of the principles expressed by the Ten Commandments. The meaning of these Ten Commandments and their relationship with the case laws will be the focus of chapter eight. Here we will consider the background to these laws in the ancient Near East.

First, we should be clear that the time of Moses was not the first time the people of God heard God's will concerning their behavior.[3] The commandment "You must not murder" (Ex 20:5) did not prohibit the illicit taking of life for the first time. Ages before Moses, when Cain

---

[3]Christopher J. H. Wright, *Old Testament Ethics for the People of God* (Downers Grove, Ill.: InterVarsity Press, 2004), p. 283, points to Genesis 26:4-5 ("because Abraham obeyed me and kept my requirements, my commands, my decrees and my laws") as an indication "that the basic content and thrust of the law, though not yet given in detail as it was at Sinai, was in principle available to and observed by Abraham."

murdered his brother Abel (Gen 4), God judged him. It was wrong for Shechem to rape Dinah (Gen 34) and for Abraham to lie (Gen 12:10-20) even before the giving of what came to be known as the seventh and ninth commandments. The significance of the Ten Commandments is not that these admonitions and prohibitions came into being for the first time. The significance has more to do with the transition of God's people from being a family to being a nation. The nation needed what was in essence a constitution and formal legal code and such was provided by the Ten Commandments and the case law.

Even so, there were changes in the expression of God's will from the period of the patriarchs and Joseph (Gen 12–50) to the time of Moses and after. A striking example of this change has to do with the laws of incest, which are applications of the commandment "You must not commit adultery" (Ex 20:14). After all, Abraham married his half sister Sarah (Gen 20:12), a relationship expressly forbidden by Leviticus 18:11; 20:17. Even so, the fact remains that the Ten Commandments do not introduce an innovation in God's will for his people. Rather it formalizes these principles for the nation as a whole.

But the background of the Ten Commandments and their associated case laws extends beyond the expression of God's will for his own people. Interestingly, God's law finds a background also in the law codes of the ancient Near East. After describing the connection between biblical and ancient Near Eastern law, we will reflect on the theological implications of the similarities and differences between the two.

Ancient Near Eastern law. The laws found in Exodus are founded in the relationship between Moses and God and thus are dated to the middle of the second millennium B.C. The recovery of ancient Near Eastern law began at the end of the nineteenth century (A.D.). Today we know that formal law codes in the region come from no later than the end of the third millennium B.C.[4]

---

[4]The following articles provide helpful background to the study of ancient Near Eastern law as well as fine bibliographies for further research. All of them come from *Civilizations of the Ancient Near East*, ed. J. Sasson (Peabody, Mass.: Hendrikson, 2000): D. Lorton, "Legal and Social Institutions of Pharaonic Egypt," pp. 345-62; S. Greengus, "Legal

When Moses received the law on Mount Sinai, he was not the first to claim the divine realm instituted legal mandates from heaven. The earliest law codes we know about were written in Sumerian beginning with the Laws of Ur-Nammu (2112–2095 B.C.). The second oldest are the laws of Lipit-Ishtar of Isin (1934–1924 B.C.). Also preceding the law of Moses are law codes written in Akkadian (the language of the Babylonians and Assyrians), the oldest of which was the Law of Eshnunna (a city associated with Tell Asmar) probably promulgated by King Dadusha (ca. 1800 B.C.). The most famous of all ancient law codes because of its length and scope, however, was the Law of Hammurabi, the founder of the Old Babylonian dynasty (ca. 1750 B.C.). We know this law code from two ancient steles that were erected in the ancient cities of Sippar and Babylon as well as a number of copies on clay tablets. At the top of the stele is a pictorial representation of the Shamash, the god of the sun and justice, presenting the law to the king. Later Mesopotamian laws are also known from the Middle Assyrian (late second millennium) and Neo-Babylonian (626–539 B.C.) periods.

While Mesopotamian law is the best known of the law codes of Israel's neighbors, there are also others, including both Egyptian and Hittite law. Clearly, the Ten Commandments did not appear in a cultural vacuum. Many of these law codes precede Moses' time. What relationship, if any, do the laws of Exodus have with these extra-biblical laws?

General similarities. As we compare biblical law, and in particular the Book of the Covenant (Ex 19–24), we should not be surprised to discover similarities. Nations need law in order to exist. They provide the rules and regulations that allow people to exist in relatively peaceful harmony. These rules and regulations require associated punishments to induce citizens to act in a way that enhances community life even at the expense of self-interest. In addition, there is nothing remarkable about the fact that all the people of the ancient Near East believed that their laws derived from heaven. The idea that humans enter freely into

and Social Institutions of Ancient Mesopotamia," pp. 469-84; H. A. Hoffner Jr., "Legal and Social Institutions of Hittite Anatolia," pp. 555-69; H. Avalos, "Legal and Social Institutions in Canaan and Ancient Israel," pp. 615-31.

a social compact based on laws agreed upon by people awaits the modern period. The difference here, of course, is in the identification of the deity that gave the law to humans. Non-Israelites of the day worshiped many gods (polytheism), but even so it was typically one god who was responsible for the maintenance of social order through law. Above, for instance, we named Shamash, the sun god, as the one pictured giving his law to King Hammurabi. The sun god was thought fitting because the sun illuminates the darkness and through its heat can also punish the evildoer.

We might be a bit more surprised to recognize that many of the values of biblical laws are also found in ancient Near Eastern law. Kings of the ancient Near East picture themselves as those who are interested in the establishment of justice in the land. They characterize themselves as those who take care of the disenfranchised. Like the law of the Old Testament (Ex 22:22-24), they take pride in claiming that they watch out for the interests of widows, orphans, and others who are unable to care for themselves (Prologue to Code of Ur-Nammu: "The orphan was not delivered up to the rich man; the widow was not delivered up to the mighty man; the man of one shekel was not delivered up to the man of one mina"[5]). The major Mesopotamian law codes are also vitally concerned to regulate fair trade practices and so they provide penalties against merchants who cheat in weights and measurements.

In general we can say that the laws of the ancient Near East are not all that different from the biblical laws when we consider the general principles that regulate human interaction as expressed by the fifth to the ninth commandments. They too have laws that protect parents' authority over children and prohibit murder, adultery, theft and lying.

Yet a further similarity has to do with the form of the law "codes" and the style in which the laws were written. The similarity has to do with the fact that they are not really codes at all, if that term is taken to indicate a systematic and exhaustive presentation of the laws of the land. In

---

[5]J. J. Finkelstein, "The Laws of Ur-Nammu," in *Ancient Near Eastern Texts Relating to the Old Testament with Supplement*, ed. J. B. Pritchard (Princeton: Princeton University Press, 1969), p. 524.

the first place, the laws are not exhaustive. One can think of legal situations that are not specifically covered by a law: treason, abortion, certain forms of arson, and the list could go on and on. Indeed, the suggestion has been made to refer to these ancient Near Eastern, including biblical, laws as collections rather than codes.[6] In the second place, they are not systematic. A quick read through Exodus 20–23 will convince readers that the material does not yield a tight outline, though some laws that concern the same general subject are together.

In terms of the form of the laws themselves, the ancient Near Eastern collections are almost exclusively in the form of case law ("if . . . then") referring to a specific situation:

> *If a craftsman takes a young child to rear and then teaches him his craft, he will not be reclaimed. (Law 188 in the Code of Hammurabi)*[7]

This case law format is similar to the vast majority of law in the Book of the Covenant (Ex 19–24), but dissimilar from the form of the Ten Commandments, which are in the form of general ethical principles, for example "You must not murder" (Ex 20:13).[8] Indeed, the structure of the book of the covenant, which has the Ten Commandments at the beginning, followed by the case law, which are specific applications of these general principles (see explanation in chapter 8), is unprecedented in the ancient Near East.

Specific similarities. Again, we should not be surprised by the general similarities such as those named above. It would be hard to imagine a society that did not have laws that protected the life and property of its citizens. What is more surprising is the appearance of specific laws whose similarity is more precise, thus suggesting something more than the independent development of general ethical principles.

---

[6]See M. J. Selman, "Law," in *Dictionary of the Old Testament: The Pentateuch*, ed. T. Desmond Alexander and David W. Baker (Downers Grove, Ill.: InterVarsity Press, 2003), p. 500.

[7]Translation by M. Roth in *Context of Scripture*, vol. 2, ed. W. W. Hallo and K. Lawson Younger (Leiden: Brill, 1997), p. 347.

[8]It is true that such general ethical principles can be found in treaty documents, but not in legal codes.

The goring ox law is a prime example of this type of similarity. Exodus 21:28-32 is a case law that demonstrates how the sixth commandment applies in the event that an ox gores and kills a person. It is not necessary to get into all the details of this law in order to make our point. In general though, the first time an ox gores a person, the ox must be stoned. If the ox is not killed and lives to gore a second individual, then both ox and its owner will be stoned. The law makes sense since the owner of a proven dangerous animal assumes responsibility for its actions since he did not have it killed.

The following laws are from the Code of Eshnunna and the later Code of Hammurabi:

> *If an ox gores another ox and thus causes its death, the two ox-owners shall divide the value of the living ox and the carcass of the dead ox. If an ox is a gorer and the ward authorities so notify its owner, but he fails to keep his ox in check, the owner of the ox shall weigh and deliver 40 shekels of silver. If it gores a slave and thus causes his death, he shall weigh and deliver 15 shekels of silver.* (Eshnunna, laws 53-55)[9]

> *If an ox gores to death a man while it is passing through the streets, that case has no basis for a claim. If a man's ox is a known gorer, and the authorities of his city quarter notify him that it is a known gorer, but he does not blunt (?) its horns or control his ox, and that ox gores to death a member of the awilu-class, he (the owner) shall give 30 shekels of silver. If it is a man's slave (who is fatally gored), he shall give 20 shekels of silver.* (Code of Hammurabi, laws 250-252)

J. J. Finkelstein, the man who studied these laws more closely than anyone, concluded, rightly in my opinion, that "we are confronted here not with independent developments, but with a single, organically interrelated, literary tradition." He also believed that the biblical goring ox law "must have been dependent upon their literary Mesopotamian prototypes" since the actual frequency with which oxen gored humans precluded the idea that the laws would rise spontaneously in these different cultures.[10]

---

[9] Translation by M. Roth, *Context of Scripture*, 2:335.

[10] J. J. Finkelstein, *The Ox That Gored* (Philadelphia: American Philosophical Society, 1981).

I believe that the similarities here indicate that this law is an example of a law that was written in the light of earlier ancient Near Eastern legal tradition. After all, the same principle could have been enunciated in a different matter. This case law is not just applicable to a dangerous ox, but would have been used by Israelite judges to guide their decisions concerning the culpability of an owner of a dangerous dog, ram or other animal. It is likely that the Israelites' law similarly describes an ox rather than any other animal (or just animals in general) because of the precursor laws of the ancient Near East.[11]

Attentive readers might already understand the theological issue that is raised by this comment. The Bible says that the law (Ten Commandments and the case law) was given by God from heaven, not written by humans in consultation with traditional law. Further thought, however, will lead to the realization that the true and wise God of the Bible articulated his will in a manner that was recognizable to his people. He expressed his will through the human instrument of a law code and at times expressed his specific will through the use of a law that was known elsewhere in the ancient Near East. The uniqueness of biblical law is not based on the fact that its ethic and formulation cannot be found elsewhere. Human beings, including ancient Near Eastern people like those that produced these ancient law codes, were totally sinful, but that meant they were sinful in every aspect of their life. If the first were true, rather than the second, then they would not be able to formulate an ethical system of laws. Another way of viewing the similarity is that they were not totally misshapen by their sin, they could still recognize principles by which they should live in a harmonious way. To use the language of systematic theology, while they were not the recipients of God's special grace that would restore a relationship with him, God still demonstrated his common grace toward them.

While all this is true, there are also contrasts to be drawn between bibli-

---

[11]It is indeed true that the biblical law mandates death for the owner in the case of a second case of goring while the Mesopotamian laws require only a fine of varying expense depending on the social class of the victim. Perhaps this reflects a higher regard for life in the biblical text.

cal and ancient Near Eastern law. It is to that subject that we now turn.

Contrasts. While biblical law shares features with the laws of the broader ancient Near East, there are also demonstrable differences. Our purpose here is not to be exhaustive but suggestive.

The most significant difference concerns the origin of the law. Yes, all the law codes place the origin of law in the heavenly realm. The difference has to do with the deity responsible for law. Israel recognized only Yahweh as their God, while the other peoples of the ancient Near East were polytheists. True, they thought that one of their gods specialized in law giving, but that God was not Yahweh but some figment of their imagination. Thus, the first difference is Israel's belief that it was Yahweh who gave the law to Moses.

A second significant difference is also connected to Israel's religion. It is striking that the other ancient Near Eastern codes do not treat matters of religion. They regulate human behavior, but not the relationship between people and their deities. Of course, Israelite laws treat both. Indeed, the first four of the Ten Commandments speak to the divine–human relationship and many laws in Exodus (as well as Leviticus—Deuteronomy) mandate matters concerning worship.

Yet another difference has to do with the form of the law. The goring ox law of Exodus compares well with the content of the goring ox laws of Mesopotamia. They also share the same basic form; they are case laws. They share a similar grammatical structure, that of a conditional statement with a protasis ("if") followed by an apodosis ("then"). While the various law codes share this formal similarity, there is nothing quite like the Ten Commandments in the other ancient law codes. The Ten Commandments differ from the case laws by their formulation as general ethical principles. Old Testament scholars refer to this form as apodictic law. As we will observe in chapter seven, the Ten Commandments provide the general ethical principles that are then applied to specific situations in the case law. One can see the true God's wisdom in articulating his will in the form of such general principles so they can be applied to evolving situations as time progresses (see chapter 8).

The ancient Near Eastern codes are interested in regulating behavior.

The biblical code is as well. However, the biblical code uniquely goes deeper than the others. This is accomplished by the tenth commandment, the law against coveting. God is not just interested in proper behavior, but also in terms of a proper heart.

THE ANCIENT NEAR EASTERN BACKGROUND OF THE TABERNACLE

Ancient Near Eastern background study has served a somewhat different purpose in regards to the tabernacle tradition of Exodus 25–40. As we saw above, sometimes the ancient Near Eastern background can enlarge or enrich our understanding of the biblical text. Upon occasion, it can also be marshaled to support the idea of the veracity of the text. As we will comment below (see chapter 5), archaeology is not in the business of either proving or disproving a text tradition. Nevertheless, it can offer support or raise questions about the claims of a text.

Since the second half of the nineteenth century, the description of the tabernacle as a portable shrine during the premonarchic period has been questioned by scholars.[12] The idea of an ornate, expensive portable shrine used for religious purposes seemed out of place with this early historical setting (second half of the second millennium B.C.). Of course, such a view is popular today with many scholars, most notably the so-called minimalists (see pp. 83-84) who believe that much of the Bible is the later imaginative work of people who lived in the first millennium. Wellhausen's views were not as radical as the minimalists, since he believed, based on some parallels between the temple and the tabernacle, that the latter was a retrojection of the temple back to the period of wandering.

In response, other scholars have responded by citing ancient Near Eastern evidence of ornate tent structures, including those used for ritual purposes, which comes from the time of the biblical tabernacle and even before. Recently, Kenneth Kitchen, the prominent Egyptologist, has summarized the evidence that is available to us and cited the rele-

---

[12]Many would point to J. Wellhausen, *Prolegomena to the History of Israel* (1883; reprint, Atlanta: Scholars Press, 1994), as the origin of the idea.

vant scholarly literature.[13] The earliest relevant material comes from paintings on tomb walls of tabernacle-like structures that served as locations for mummification (1st Dynasty: ca. 3000–2800 B.C.). Also, from two or three centuries later (4th Dynasty), the pyramid building king Khufu's mother, Herepheres, had what Kitchen calls a "secular tabernacle" structure covering her bedroom furniture in her tomb.[14] He concludes his analysis of the third millennium material by concluding that "most of the biblical tabernacle's technology was literally as 'old as the Pyramids,' in fact older."[15]

In the next millennium, Kitchen refers to evidence from the sites of Mari and Ugarit, moving closer to the world of the Bible, both in terms of time and culture. Citing evidence from the work of Dan Fleming, he notes the evidence for "large tents over wooden frames set in socketed bases" that "were used for both ritual and royal purposes at Mari, still half a millennium before any Moses."[16] The Ugaritic texts, from the thirteenth century B.C. but based on earlier oral compositions, refer to the gods living in tents. Also in the second millennium (just after the reign of Rameses V [ca. 1147–1143 B.C.]) archaeologists have recovered a Midianite tabernacle at Timna, a copper mining town abandoned by the Egyptians.

These arguments go a considerable distance in response to the claim that the tabernacle was a later imaginative creation. The presence of third and second millennium ornate text shrines in Egypt, Mari, Ugarit, and Midian provides justification for believing that the Israelites too could have worshiped their God in a tabernacle.

CONCLUSION

Again, the above connections between the book of Exodus and its broader ancient Near Eastern background are only illustrative. Many

---

[13]K. Kitchen, *The Reliability of the Old Testament* (Grand Rapids: Eerdmans, 2003), pp. 274-83. Also helpful is the article by R. Averbeck, "Tabernacle," in *Dictionary of the Old Testament: The Pentateuch*, ed. T. Desmond Alexander and David W. Baker (Downers Grove, Ill.: InterVarsity Press, 2003), pp. 807-27.

[14]Kitchen, *Reliability*, p. 276.

[15]Ibid.

[16]Ibid, p. 277.

other examples of helpful connections could be drawn. Of course, as exemplified by our analysis above, the sensitive interpreter has to be aware of differences within the similarities. Furthermore, we must be careful not to leap to conclusions about any kind of direct dependence between the material, though sometimes the evidence leans in that direction (as with the goring ox law).

In any case, while due caution should be exercised, the study of the ancient Near Eastern background of biblical books proves to be illuminating. Further implications of these connections as well as others will be examined in the chapters that follow.

QUESTIONS FOR DISCUSSION

1. Do you find it surprising that the book of Exodus has a number of similarities with its ancient Near Eastern environment? Why or why not?

2. How would you describe the uniqueness of the book of Exodus over against the literature of its neighbors?

3. What role does faith have in describing the connection between the biblical text and similar ancient Near Eastern texts?

4. It takes research and dependence on specialists today to even recover the ancient Near Eastern materials. Does this mean that lay people can't understand the Bible without expert help? Why or why not?

FOR FURTHER READING

Greengus, S. "Legal and Social Institutions of Ancient Mesopotamia," pp. 469-83. In *Civilizations of the Ancient Near East,* edited by J. Sasson. Peabody, Mass.: Hendrickson, 2000.

Hoffner, H. A., Jr. "Legal and Social Institutions of Hittite Anatolia," pp. 555-69. In *Civilizations of the Ancient Near East,* edited by J. Sasson. Peabody, Mass.: Hendrickson, 2000.

Lorton, D. "Legal and Social Institutions of Pharaonic Egypt," pp. 345-62. In *Civilizations of the Ancient Near East,* edited by J. Sasson. Peabody, Mass.: Hendrickson, 2000.

Sparks, K. *Ancient Texts for the Study of the Hebrew Bible: A Guide to the Background Literature.* Peabody, Mass.: Hendrickson, 2005.

Walton, John H. *Ancient Near Eastern Thought and the Old Testament: Introducing the Conceptual World of the Hebrew Bible.* Grand Rapids: Baker, 2006.

Walton, John H., Victor H. Matthews, and Mark W. Chavalas. *The IVP Bible Background Commentary: Old Testament.* Downers Grove, Ill.: InterVarsity Press, 2000.

The ancient Near Eastern Texts that are discussed above (and many others that are relevant to the study of the Bible) may be found in a number of places, but the two most accessible are

Ancient Near Eastern Texts Relating to the Old Testament with Supplement (commonly referred to as ANET), edited by J. B. Pritchard. Princeton: Princeton University Press, 1969.

Context of Scripture (commonly abbreviated COS). 3 vols, edited by W. W. Hallo and K. L. Younger Jr. Leiden: E. J. Brill, 1997-2002.

FIVE

EVIDENCE FOR THE EXODUS EVENT

The exodus is the high point of the salvation history of the Old Testament. The exodus fueled Israel's self-identity as the chosen people of God. It was part of the complex of redemptive events that transformed them from a family of God to a nation of God. The exodus was a salvation event that was epitomized by the crossing of the *Yam Suf*, commonly, but probably incorrectly, translated Red Sea (Ex 14–15). This Sea crossing not only provided rescue for threatened Israel but also simultaneously judged her enemies. The special status of this rescue is underlined by the fact that Moses and his people found themselves in an impossible situation with the Sea on one side and an embarrassed and angry Pharaoh and his elite chariot troops on the other. There was no human avenue of escape. They were cut off, but God did the impossible, opened the Sea and allowed them to escape. And then he closed the Sea to execute judgment on their enemies. The Exodus gave Israel its self-identity. From such a description we can recognize that it is hard to underestimate the importance of the Exodus event.

But did it happen and does it matter whether or not it happened?

We begin with an assessment of the current state of the historical evidence in regard to the Exodus.

We must admit that there is no direct evidence outside of the Bible for the exodus. There is no mention of Israel or Moses in Egyptian sources, for instance. Purported discoveries of the wheels of Pharaoh's chariots beside the Red Sea are misleading if not fraudulent (see further below).[1]

Of course, we can immediately recognize why there is such an absence. We rarely hear of Egyptian defeats from Egyptian sources and this event would have been particularly embarrassing to Egypt. This is not the type of event that they would want to remember or memorialize on a large stone monument or on tomb walls.

What we do have on tomb walls, however, does show that Semitic peoples were engaged in slave labor in the 2nd millennium in Egypt. As early as the reign of Thutmosis III around 1460 B.C. we have scenes of foreigners who are making bricks for the temple of Amun in Thebes for instance. This is one example of some indirect evidence that can be marshaled to make the account of the Exodus sound reasonable.[2] In this context, we should also note that the first extrabiblical evidence for the existence of Israel as a people in Egypt comes from the very end of the thirteenth century B.C. in a victory monument of Pharaoh Merneptah (also known as the Israel stele), which mentions Israel as a vanquished enemy.[3]

However, there are further problems connected to the archaeology of both Egypt and Palestine as it relates to the exodus and the closely related conquest. Here we can only be illustrative rather than exhaustive, but in a word the results of archaeological research over the past one hundred years do not fit easily with the biblical description of the exodus and conquest.

The problem extends to the issue of the date of the conquest. This problem is raised on two levels. For one, the chronological information that we do get in the Bible are relative dates, not absolute dates and we

---

[1]For a decisive debunking of this and other sensationalist claims that archaeology proves the Bible, see E. Cline, *From Eden to Exile: Unraveling the Mysteries of the Bible* (Washington, D.C.: National Geographic, 2007).

[2]For a full and excellent presentation of the indirect evidence for the Exodus event, see J. Hoffmeier, *Israel in Egypt: The Evidence for the Authenticity of the Exodus Tradition* (New York: Oxford University Press, 1997). Figures 8 and 9 in this book reproduce the scene of the Asiatic laborers making bricks.

[3]For which see W. W. Hallo and K. L. Younger Jr., eds., *Context of Scripture* (Leiden: Brill, 2000), 2:40-41.

have to translate them to our system. As we will see, we also have to reckon with the possibility that the dates we are given are not literal numbers but symbolic. And then second, the biblical text does not provide the name of the Pharaoh.

Beginning with the second issue, imagine how many of our issues would be resolved if the narrative had named the Pharaoh! Thutmosis or Rameses, or perhaps another, but the account does not give us a name and its absence raises the question, why not? Hoffmeier has been helpful in responding to this issue by pointing out that it is likely that the biblical account is mimicking the Egyptian practice of not naming and thus glorifying an enemy.[4]

Now on to the first issue: How do biblical scholars convert the relative dates of the Bible into absolute dates? After all, in the Bible we do not have an absolute dating system like our contemporary B.C. (B.C.E.) and A.D. (C.E.) system. Events are recorded using a relative dating system. The same is true when it comes to dating the Exodus. The main text is 1 Kings 6:1: "It was in midspring, in the month of Ziv, during the fourth year of Solomon's reign, that he began to construct the Temple of the Lord. This was 480 years after the people of Israel were rescued from their slavery in the land of Egypt."

The text places the exodus four hundred and eighty years before the fourth year of Solomon, the year he began to construct the temple. Thus, if we can determine the date of the fourth year of Solomon, theoretically at least, we could establish an absolute date for the exodus.

But, if all the dates in the Bible are relative, how can we transition to an absolute date?

We begin by turning our attention to chronological texts from Assyria, the most important of which is the Assyrian Eponym Canon (AEC), a dating system that covers the years 910–612 B.C. The Eponym Canon does not provide absolute dates on the surface; it lists years by the names of a *limu* (important official) or king and associates that year with a significant event that occurred during that year. These events

---

[4]Hoffmeier, *Israel in Egypt*, pp. 109, 112.

include statements about war, flooding and astronomical phenomenon, including eclipses. Since eclipses occur at regular and predictable times, astronomers today can calculate when they occurred in antiquity in Assyria (ancient northern Iraq) and thus provide an absolute date for the *limu.* An eclipse of the sun is mentioned during the "eponymate of Barsagale, of Guzan." This event can be dated to 763 B.C. This date provides a center from which other relative dates can be determined. By the use of the AEC in comparison with other Assyrian historical texts that mention Israel (i.e., the Black Oblelisk that mentions the Assyrian king Shalmaneser making Jehu of Israel pay tribute), scholars can assign an absolute date to certain biblical events. Once some biblical events are dated this way, the relative dates can be converted into absolute dates.

Without going through all the details, by proceeding in this fashion it is possible to situate the fourth year of Solomon to 966 B.C., give or take a few years. If so, then by adding 480 years to 966, we end up with an approximate date of the exodus in the middle of the fifteenth century B.C.[5]

Other biblical texts support this date, but they are not as precise or dependable as 1 Kings 6:1. For instance, in his negotiations with the Ammonites concerning the occupation of land in the Transjordan region, Jephthah makes the argument that "Israel has been living here for 300 years, inhabiting Heshbon and its surrounding settlements, all the way to Aroer and its settlements, and in all the towns along the Arnon River. Why have you made no effort to recover it before now?" (Judg 11:26).

Jephthah here refers to the taking of this region in the time just before the conquest of Palestine, which of course takes place forty years after the exodus. The chronology of Judges does not allow us to specifically date the time of Jephthah, though a period of 300 years certainly makes more sense of a fifteenth-century exodus followed by the conquest than its leading rival date of the thirteenth century, to be described below.

THE PROBLEM WITH A FIFTEENTH-CENTURY DATE
On the surface at least the biblical text is clear and self-consistent, point-

[5]See F. H. Cryer, "Chronology: Issues and Problems," in *Civilizations of the Ancient Near East,* vol. 2, ed. J. Sasson (Peabody, Mass.: Hendrickson, 1995), pp. 651-64.

ing to the fifteenth century B.C. The problem arises not with the Bible, but rather with the archaeological evidence. In a word, the conclusions of archaeologists working in the second half of the twentieth century and into the present century do not support the biblical picture.[6] In this section, we will present the problems and respond to them in a section to follow.

The issues surround (1) problems as to the names and identification of the cities Exodus 1:11 names as the location of Israel's forced labor; and (2) archaeological evidence from the cities defeated by Joshua during the conquest.

Pithom and Rameses. According to Exodus 1:11: "They appointed brutal slave drivers over them, hoping to wear them down with crushing labor. They forced them to build the cities of Pithom and Rameses as supply centers for the king."

The first problem for a fifteenth-century date is the name of the second city: Rameses.[7] The name of this city derives from a royal name known from the 18th dynasty, beginning in the late fourteenth/early thirteenth century B.C. As we will observe later, one of the leading contenders for the Pharaoh of the Exodus is Rameses II (1279–1213 B.C.).

More telling, since we could explain the name as postmosaic,[8] is the

---

[6]Many books may be cited as supporting this conclusion, but W. G. Dever's *Who Were the Early Israelites and Where Did They Come From?* (Grand Rapids: Eerdmans, 2003) may be taken as a recent representative.

[7]Exodus 1:11 spells the name Raamses, though other occurrences of the name in the Bible (Gen 47:11; Ex 12:37; Num 33:3, 5) spell it Rameses.

[8]It is clear that additions and updates were made to the Pentateuch during the period of canon formation, the most famous of which is the account of Moses' death in Deuteronomy 34. Indeed, the reference to Rameses in Genesis 47:11 is such an updating, no matter when one dates the Exodus. Hoffmeier's arguments against the idea that this is a postmosaic updating ("What is the Biblical Date for the Exodus? A Response to Bryant Wood," *Journal of the Evangelical Theological Society* 50 [2007]: 223-24) has been successfully answered by B. Wood, "The Biblical Date for the Exodus is 1446 BC: A Response to James Hoffmeier," *Journal of the Evangelical Theological Society* 50 [2007]: 250-53). In a most peculiar article, R. Vasholz ("On the Dating of the Exodus," *Presbyterion* 32 [2006]: 111-13) has argued that the city was actually named Rameses in the fifteenth century. His view has been effectively undermined by J. Hoffmeier, "Rameses of the Exodus Narratives Is the 13th Century B.C. Royal Ramesside Residence," *Trinity Journal* 28 (2007): 1-8.

second problem that concerns the dating of the archaeological site associated with Rameses.[9] Consensus now is that Rameses should be associated with Pi-Rameses and identified with Qantir (Tell el-Daba'a).[10] Kitchen is representative of the view that the archaeology of Qantir settles the question of the date of the Exodus, since, in his opinion, the archaeological results only point to the thirteenth century B.C.. Kitchen, though aware of some remains pointing to the reign of Seti I (1294–1279 B.C.),[11] points to massive building during the reign of Rameses II. He also emphasizes the short-lived nature of the settlement here. Due to a change in the course of the Nile, Qantir was soon abandoned, and by the eleventh century the center of power (as well as much of the stone and other remains of Qantir) was moved to Tanis (Zoan).

The archaeology of the conquest. Another problem for the fifteenth century date has to do with the date of the conquest, which of course bears on the date of the exodus since the biblical record reports the conquest began forty years after the exodus.

Close reading of the book of Joshua indicates that widespread destruction of urban centers did not occur. [12] Only Jericho, Ai and Hazor were said to be burned during Joshua's campaign, and most of the other victories took place on the open battlefield. Thus, the absence of burn layers throughout Palestine dated to this period is not disturbing. However, many of the sites said to have been in existence according to the

---

[9]The archaeological evidence for Tel er-Retebe, often identified as Pithom, is not problematic for either the early or the late date of the exodus.

[10]According to K. Kitchen ("Egypt, Egyptians," in *The Dictionary of the Old Testament: Pentateuch*, ed. T. Desmond Alexander and David W. Baker [Downers Grove, Ill.: InterVarsity Press, 2003], p. 210): "Beyond any serious doubt, Raamses is Pi-Ramesses, the once vast Delta residence-city built by Ramesses II (1279–1213 B.C.), marked by ruin-fields that extend for almost four miles north to south and nearly two miles west to east, centered on Qantir (Tell el-Dab'a), a dozen miles or so south of Tanis (Zoan)."

[11]Though more recently, M. Bietak, the archaeologist of the site, has reported remains of a citadel and storage facility from the time of Thutmosis III during the 18th Dynasty (mid-15th century B.C.), using bricks from an even earlier citadel from the Hyksos period. See M. Bietak, "Dab'a Tell Ed-," in *The Oxford Encyclopedia of Ancient Egypt*, ed. D. B. Redford (Oxford: Oxford University Press, 2001), p. 353.

[12]For a more detailed account of the evidence, as well as a rejoinder to many of the conclusions of archaeologists, see I. Provan, V. P. Long and T. Longman, *A Biblical History of Israel* (Louisville: Westminster John Knox, 2003), pp. 174-89.

exodus and conquest accounts do not show signs of habitation during the Late Bronze Age (c. 1550–1200 B.C.), the period in which the events purportedly took place.

Let's take a look, for instance, at Jericho. Of course, Jericho was Israel's first great victory after crossing the Jordan River. The biblical text describes it as a major city with massive walls. When John Garstang, the British archaeologist, dug at Tell es-Sultan, universally recognized as ancient Jericho, in the 1930's, he claims to have discovered the walls that fell at the time of Jericho. However, from 1952–1958, a new archaeological investigation was launched by Kathleen Kenyon, also a British archaeologist. Her conclusions were radically different from Garstang's. According to her work, Jericho shows signs of existing before the fifteenth century and afterward, but not at the time of the conquest. Her conclusions were driven largely by the lack of a certain type of ceramic pottery, imported Cypriot bichrome ware, that was characteristic of the period. Its lack indicated to her that no one lived at Tell es-Sultan at that time.

Ai proved to be another problem for those who want to date the exodus/conquest to the late fifteenth century. Ai means "dump" or "ruin" in Hebrew and so it is often associated with a modern archaeological site that has the name Khirbet et-Tell, et-Tell being Arabic for "the ruin." It is located near Beiten, often associated with the ancient city of Bethel, which the Bible tells us was near ancient Ai. Archaeologists who have studied the remains at this site note that there is no evidence of occupation for the period between 2400–1200 B.C.[13] Thus, according to this interpretation of the archaeological evidence, the biblical picture must be wrong in terms of date or substance.

REDATING THE EXODUS EVENT

As we will describe below, the problematic archaeological evidence has led many scholars to abandon or modify the idea of the exodus and the conquest as explanations for how Israel comes into being in the land of

---

[13]B. S. J. Isserlin, *The Israelites* (New York: Thames and Hudson, 1998), p. 57.

Palestine. For now, we will focus on those scholars who are persuaded by the archaeological evidence but continue to believe that the exodus and conquest actually happened. In a word, they recalibrate the biblical statements about date.

The most passionate recent defenders of the following position are Kenneth Kitchen and James Hoffmeier,[14] both hold a high view of Scripture and are eminent Egyptologists. They propose that the 480 year period between the exodus and the fourth year of Solomon (1 Kings 6:1) is not a literal but a symbolic number. The key is the fact that the number is divisible by 40, which represents a generation. After all, the wilderness wandering period was forty years, the time for the first generation to die and for a second generation to rise in its place. So 480 stands for 12 generations.[15]

However, while 40 is a symbolic number for a generation, it is not the actual, typical age when people start having children and thus begin the next generation. They suggest that 25 is the actual number of a generation. Thus, to get the real number of years represented by the number 480, we must multiply 12 times 25. The result is 300, which added to 966 B.C. (the 4th year of Solomon, give or take) points to 1266, or the thirteenth century B.C. Such a date works much better with the results of archaeology.

While this solution is tenable, it does have a tone of desperation around it. It takes a bit of imagination to make the number work. Imagination may be what is called for, but, on the other hand, perhaps the conflict between archaeology and the biblical evidence should lead us in the opposite direction. Rather than rereading the biblical text, perhaps we should reread the archaeological material.

---

[14]See the recent interchange between James Hoffmeier ("What Is the Biblical Date? A Response to Bryant Wood," *JETS* 50 [2007]: 225-47) and the rejoinder, defending the early date, by Bryant Wood ("The Biblical Date for the Exodus is 1446 BC: A Response to James Hoffmeier," *JETS* [2007]: 249-58).

[15]N. Sarna, *Exploring Exodus: The Origins of Biblical Israel* (New York: Schocken, 1996), p. 9, also points out that there are approximately 480 years from Solonon's fourth year until the Cyrus decree that leads to the second temple generation in 538 B.C. Thus, he suggests that the writer intends to mark the beginning of the construction of the second temple as the middle point of Israel's chronology.

REREADING THE ARCHAEOLOGICAL MATERIAL

The metaphor of reading and rereading the archaeological remains is intentionally chosen. Many lay people and minimalists (see below) have the mistaken impression that archaeology is a science that involves no or minimal interpretation, contrasting with the study of the Bible which everyone recognizes demands interpretation. While archaeology utilizes some methods of study that are scientific (and science itself involves interpretation), the understanding of mute archaeological remains is a hermeneutical (interpretive) task just like the study of the Bible. Archaeological remains are amenable to more than one interpretation.

Can the materials associated with the dating of the Egyptian store cities and the cities of the conquest be reread in a way that conforms to a fifteenth-century date of the conquest?

In a now classic and controversial[16] study published in 1978, J. J. Bimson argued that there was a way to interpret the archaeological materials that is conducive to a fifteenth century date of the exodus.[17]

The details of his arguments cannot be presented here, but the broad outline of his reinterpretation is as follows:

According to a traditional reading of the archaeological work done in the twentieth century in Palestine, the end of the Middle Bronze Age in Palestine (ca. 1550 B.C.) witnessed the destruction of many cities. This destruction has been attributed to Egyptian armies that moved into Palestine in pursuit of fleeing Hyksos, a Semitic group that had dominated Egypt for about one hundred years. Bimson, however, points out that there is no textual or artifactual reason to associate the destruction of these cities with the fleeing Hyksos. Indeed, the texts speak of a pursuit only as far as Sharuhen in southern Palestine and the Egyptians took that city only after a three-year siege.[18]

---

[16]B. Halpern, "Radical Exodus Redating Fatally Flawed," *Biblical Archaeology Review* 13 (1987): 56-61.

[17]J. J. Bimson, *Redating the Exodus and Conquest* (Sheffield: University of Sheffield Press, 1978).

[18]Some want to argue that these northern Palestinian cities were destroyed later by Thutmosis III and indeed we have textual evidence of this pharaoh's campaigns into north-

Bimson thus questions dating the destruction of these cities to the sixteenth century and their association with the Hyksos. He presents the view that they should rather be placed in the fifteenth century and associated with the Hebrews.

Other scholars have also joined the effort of reassessing archaeological interpretations that have dominated the field for years. Bryant Wood, for instance, has questioned Kathleen Kenyon's chronology of Jericho based on ceramics. [19]

Bimson appropriately does not insist that his interpretation is definitely the right one, but what he does effectively demonstrate, even if certain aspects of his theory can be shown to be wrong, is that archaeology is amenable to more than one reading or interpretation. In my opinion, it is utterly wrong-minded to divorce textual evidence from archaeological evidence.[20] Many scholars today operate with a method that says archaeology should not be interpreted in the light of the biblical text but rather independently. I think that archaeology should be done in the light of textual records (biblical or otherwise). Not that archaeology should be misread to make it fit the biblical record, but rather the archaeologist and historian should ask if the material that we have fits with the biblical text. Bimson's conclusions are an example of this. Palestinian cities show a destruction level that, in light of what we know from texts, could be associated with the Hyksos or the Israelites. However, those texts say nothing about destruction of cities to the north of Sharuhen, but do inform us that Joshua destroyed certain cities. Thus, why not interpret the archaeology in that direction?

Of course, this would put the emergence of Israel at the start of the

---

ern Palestine. However, we have no evidence that he destroyed all the cities on his list. Rather he may have been making a show of force as he collected tribute.

[19]B. Wood, "Did the Israelites Conquer Jericho? A New Look at the Archaeological Evidence," *Biblical Archaeology Review* 16 (1990): 44-58.

[20]John Walton, "Exodus, Date of," in *Dictionary of the Old Testament: Pentateuch*, ed. T. Desmond Alexander and David W. Baker (Downers Grove, Ill.: InterVarsity Press, 2003), pp. 268-69, makes the point very clearly: "From the above discussions it is evident that the complexity of this issue derives from the need to juxtapose biblical, historical and archaeological data to one another. When the data are not easily reconciled, which data hold priority?"

Late Bronze Age rather than the Iron Age. Neither transition provides strong evidence for a significant break in culture that some expect when a foreign intruding culture (Israelite) replaces the resident culture (Canaanite). Thus, a number of scholars argue that what we call Israelite is really an inner-Canaanite development.[21] That is, there are no external intruders. However, it is questionable whether an intrusive migratory people would enter the land and establish a discernably different material culture. Perhaps they adapted their pot-making to Canaanite pot-making techniques. They likely used the cisterns and other technologies of the Canaanites. Indeed, Deuteronomy 6:10b-11 warns the Israelites not to forget God who will give them a land "with large, flourishing cities you did not build. The houses will be richly stocked with goods you did not produce. You will draw water from cisterns you did not dig, and you will eat from vineyards and olive trees you did not plant." Perhaps if the list went on it would include, "pots you did not make . . ." In addition, in a fascinating article, Millard points out that many invasions that are well known from textual witness bear no archaeological trace, including the Amorite invasion of the Third Dynasty of Ur around 2000 B.C., the Saxon and Norman invasion of Britain and the Arab invasion of Palestine.[22]

LATE DATE

That said, we cannot be utterly confident that the exodus and conquest took place at the early date. Though that seems the most natural reading of texts like 1 Kings 6:1, it isn't the only reading (so Kitchen, et. al.). The truth is that the archaeological data, as traditionally interpreted, fits in better with the late date. It also, of course, makes sense of the name Rameses for one of the two store cities in Exodus 1:11. However, even the late date has problems with certain archaeological facts (see Ai above).

---

[21]See Dever, *Who Were the Early Israelites?*

[22]See A. Millard, "Amorites and Israelites: Invisible Invaders," in *The Future of Biblical Archaeology: Reassessing Methodologies and Assumptions*, ed. J. K. Hoffmeier and A. Millard (Grand Rapids: Eerdmans, 2004), pp. 148-62.

CONCLUSION

Some of my readers will be frustrated by the fact that I am unable to come to a clear decision regarding the time period of the exodus and further exasperated by the idea that archaeology does not definitively support the presence of Israel in Egypt, their escape, their wilderness wanderings, or the conquest.

On the one hand, however, the truth is that the biblical record was not written in a way to satisfy all our historical questions. Not even the few chronological statements we have (i.e., 1 Kings 6:1) are uncontroversial as we convert them to our dating system.

On the other hand, archaeological evidence is not in the business of providing objective evidence one way or the other. Such evidence is open to multiple interpretations—not any interpretation, but more than one.

What can we say in conclusion? Our present day knowledge of the archaeology of Palestine and Egypt does not lead to an easy correlation with the biblical testimony of the exodus.

Why? In the first place, the biblical material is amenable to different interpretations. What the Bible intends to teach in the book of Exodus is perfectly clear. God intervened on behalf of Israel to save them from their powerful enemies in a dramatic way. However, the Bible is not perfectly clear about the precise date that this event happened. The Egyptian kings are not named (in keeping with the Egyptian practice of not naming enemies).[23] The meager chronological information that we get from 1 Kings 6:1 and Judges 11:26 is not pointing to a precise date and there is a legitimate question as to whether the number in Kings is symbolic rather than literal.

On the other hand, the archaeological material is also amenable to different interpretations. The traditional interpretation of archaeological materials is not the only possible reading. My introduction of Bimson's work intended to illustrate this point, not to argue that his interpretation is the only possible one, a claim that not even Bimson makes.[24]

---

[23]Hoffmeier, *Israel in Egypt*, pp. 111-12.
[24]See Walton, "Exodus, Date of," pp. 249-72, for a number of other possible syntheses of

That said, good archaeological arguments can be made to support both the early and the late date of the exodus and conquest (as above), though they both have abiding questions. In reaction to the present state of our knowledge, two extremes should be avoided. First, there are those like the minimalists (see below) and others who conclude that since archaeology does not prove the exodus we must reject the idea that the exodus happened. They reach this conclusion because they a priori reject the idea that the Bible itself counts as a historical testimony.[25]

The second extreme that should be avoided is the appeal of amateur archaeology or sensationalist archaeology. As one example of this phenomenon, it is not uncommon to hear the claim that Pharaoh's chariots' wheels have been discovered at the bottom of the Red Sea (the Gulf of Aqaba). An amateur archaeologist named Ron Wyatt promoted this idea through a series of church seminars. He claimed that he had seen them and had pictures to prove his contention. They were "coral encrusted." Many ministers and Christian laypeople took this as proof of the biblical account of the exodus. On the surface of it, however, the claim is ridiculous. How could one know that these wheels were from Pharaoh's army? But the claim is worse than ridiculous, it is a fraud. The supposed coral encrusted wheels are really coral wheels. In other words, some corals form wheel-like structures naturally.[26]

Another strategy to make the exodus a more palatable story is through giving it a naturalistic interpretation, the most recent example of which is Colin Humphrey's book, *The Miracles of Exodus*.[27] By miracle, he means a miracle of timing. All the events of the exodus, from the burning bush[28] to the crossing of the Sea, which happened by a strong wind

---

biblical and archaeological evidence concerning the Exodus.

[25]For a defense of the Bible as historical testimony, see I. Provan, V. P. Long and T. Longman III, *A Biblical History of Israel* (Louisville: Westminster John Knox, 2003), pp. 3-104.

[26]See Cline, *From Eden to Exile*. In a personal communication, the archaeologist Randall Younker told me that he examined the claim personally and saw the so-called wheels, confirming that they are completely composed of coral.

[27]C. Humphrey, *The Miracles of Exodus: A Scientist's Discovery of the Extraordinary Natural Causes of the Biblical Stories* (San Francisco: HarperSanFrancisco, 2003).

[28]He explains (*The Miracles of Exodus*, pp. 77-82, following quote from p. 77) that the

at the tip of the Gulf of Aqaba, can be explained by natural phenomena. This approach makes mockery of the Bible's description of what happened (see below).

The Bible claims that the exodus and the crossing of the Yam Suph actually took place and was a witness to God's power and desire to save his people. The archaeology and historical witness can be read in such a way as to conform to an understanding of either an early or a late date, though neither is without problems.

We should hope that future archaeological research will illumine matters further. One of the problems is the fact that archaeology has really only scratched the surface of the available material. Unfortunately, with a few exceptions like Jim Hoffmeier's digs in Egypt,[29] many archaeologists are no longer interested in this question, so we may not be getting a lot of new material in the near future.

QUESTIONS FOR DISCUSSION

1. How has your view of archaeology changed (or not) in reading this chapter? Can archaeology prove or disprove the Bible?

2. Does it matter whether the exodus took place in the fifteenth or thirteenth century B.C.? What is at stake theologically in this question (if anything)?

3. This chapter pointed out that there is no direct evidence that supports the biblical picture of the exodus. Is it disconcerting to think that the faith cannot be proved by a neutral presentation of evidence? Why or why not?

---

bush "was growing on top of a region containing natural gas, which is known to exist in Midian. The natural gas came up from under the bush through cracks in the rocks, was ignited either spontaneously or by lightning." He also allows for an alternative source for the gas and that is a "volcanic vent."

[29]For preliminary reports, see Hoffmeier, *Israel in Egypt*; idem., *Ancient Israel in Sinai: The Evidence for the Authenticity of the Wilderness Tradition* (Oxford: Oxford University Press, 2005); idem. "The North Sinai Archaeological Project's Excavations at Tell el-Borg (Sinai): An Example of the 'New' Biblical Archaeology?" in *The Future of Biblical Archaeology: Reassessing Methodologies and Assumptions* (Grand Rapids: Eerdmans, 2004), pp. 53-68.

FOR FURTHER READING

Bimson, J. J. *Redating the Exodus and Conquest.* Sheffield: University of Sheffield Press, 1978.

Cline, E. *From Eden to Exile: Unraveling the Mysteries of the Bible.* Washington, D.C.: National Geographic, 2007.

Dever, W. G. *Who Were the Early Israelites and Where Did They Come From?* Grand Rapids: Eerdmans, 2003.

Hoffmeier, J. *Ancient Israel in Sinai: The Evidence for the Authenticity of the Wilderness Tradition.* New York: Oxford University Press, 2005.

———. *Israel in Egypt: The Evidence for the Authenticity of the Exodus Tradition.* New York: Oxford University Press, 1997.

Hoffmeier, J., and A. Millard, eds. *The Future of Biblical Archaeology: Reassessing Methodologies and Assumptions.* Grand Rapids: Eerdmans, 2004.

Howard, D., Jr., and M. A. Grisanti, eds. *Giving the Sense: Understanding and Using Old Testament Historical Texts.* Grand Rapids: Kregel, 2003.

Provan, I., V. P. Long and T. Longman III. *A Biblical History of Israel.* Louisville: Westminster John Knox, 2003.

SIX

DOES IT MATTER
WHETHER THE SEA PARTED?

Radical challenges to the historicity of the Old Testament have dominated the scholarly discussion for the past decade and a half. A group of
loosely affiliated scholars have led the charge, questioning the historical
value of biblical narrative. They have been dubbed "minimalists" because their conclusion is that a minimum of the Old Testament story is
historically valid.[1] They argue that a new group came into Palestine in
the Persian (post-539 B.C. [for some, even the Greek, post-332 B.C.]) period for the first time. People like Zerubbabel and Sheshbazzar, Ezra and
Nehemiah weren't returning to Judah after an exile, they were coming
into the area for the very first time. In order to justify their presence in
the land, they constructed a story that told of their long occupation and
the divine gift of the land to an ancestor, Abraham, who never existed.[2]

---

[1]The minimalist approach is different than the perspective adopted by many literary
scholars of the Bible in the period of roughly 1980–1995. The latter believed that the fact
that the Bible was story meant that the question of history was unimportant. A. Berlin's
(*Poetics and Interpretation*, p. 13) comments about Abraham are representative: "Above
all, we must keep in mind that narrative is a form of representation. Abraham in Genesis
is not a real person any more than the painting of an apple is a real fruit."

[2]See P. R. Davies, *In Search of "Ancient Israel"* (Sheffield: JSOT Press, 1992); N. P. Lemche,
Ancient Israel: A New History of Israelite Society (Sheffield: JSOT Press, 1988); K. W.

The deep skepticism of the minimalists is new and not shared by the broad circle of scholars, even those who practice historical critical scholarship. Most scholars don't question the exile, the Babylonian destruction of Jerusalem, the monarchy, even Solomon and David. However, many scholars have doubted the stories that precede the time period of the rise of kingship in Israel, the exodus included.

Recently, I've noticed a trend that concerns me: fellow evangelical scholars who have questioned or doubted the historical truth of the exodus event. Granted, few have put their thoughts in print and most of my knowledge comes from personal communication and discussion, but the trend to discount the history of the exodus is present in the mind of more than a handful of such scholars. I imagine too that thoughtful seminarians, college students and pastors have wondered about the significance of the historicity of the exodus.

Such doubts arise for a variety of understandable reasons. In the previous chapter, we discussed that there is no direct evidence for the exodus outside of the Bible. Is it possible to be confident in the historicity of the exodus if Egyptian records do not mention it? Why are there no traces of the exodus story from the time period in which it purportedly took place?

Second, postmodern culture has promoted the value of story. Stories are powerful agents of transformation and vehicles of insight. Indeed, many modern and postmodern approaches to the study of literature warn against moving outside of the story itself to find its significance. Using a technical phrase, they argue against the referential function of literature. To find its meaning, one needs to enter the story and its world and not worry about anything outside of it.

In this chapter, I want to ask: Does it matter? Does it matter whether or not the exodus took place?

DOES IT MATTER?
It could be suggested that whether the exodus happened does not really

---

Whitelam, *The Invention of Ancient Israel: The Silencing of Palestinian History* (London: Routledge, 1996).

matter to our faith. The power is in the story and not in the event itself. Indeed, we only have access to the event through the story.

The past couple of decades have seen much helpful discussion about the power of story. Indeed, stories don't have to have actually happened to teach us matters of importance. Within the Bible a parable is an excellent example. Most people do not think parables record actual events. The parable of the rich man and Lazarus (Lk 16:19-31), for instance, has many life-changing lessons, even though it is unlikely that there was an actual rich man or a poor man with the name of Lazarus. The lesson of the parable is to pay heed to God speaking through the Scriptures ("Moses and the Prophets") in order to avoid a bad fate in the afterlife.

On the other hand, Paul makes it very clear that the historical nature of the resurrection is crucial to our faith: "if Christ has not been raised, then all our preaching is useless, and your faith is useless" (1 Cor 15:14). If it did not happen, Paul argues, we are all wasting our time.

However, the exodus isn't the resurrection. Certainly we cannot argue that the exodus event has the same significance to our faith as the resurrection. We are saved from our sins and death by the death and resurrection of Christ. The exodus does not have that kind of impact on our lives, nor on the lives of the Israelites at the time. The exodus is a salvation event to be sure. It saved many people from a sure death at the hands of an angry and embarrassed Egyptian Pharaoh and his army, but that is different from the kind of spiritual salvation offered by Christ, so does it really matter to us?

The question I am raising here is the same as that raised by George W. Ramsey in his interesting and honest book, *The Quest for the Historical Israel*. He posits the question in an intriguing way in regard to the conquest in the title of his last chapter: "If Jericho Was Not Razed, Is Our Faith in Vain?"[3] He suggests no. After all, unlike the resurrection of

---

[3]George W. Ramsey, *The Quest for the Historical Israel* (Louisville: John Knox, 1981). Note the helpful discussion of this book and our topic in general in V. P. Long, *The Art of Biblical History* (Grand Rapids: Zondervan, 1994), particularly chap. 3, "History and Truth: Is Historicity Important?" Also Provan, Long and Longman, *A Biblical History of Israel*, particularly chaps. 1-5.

Christ, the destruction of Jericho by Israel at the conquest does not directly affect our salvation. Our sins are not forgiven and the sting of death is not removed because the walls came tumbling down.

On the other hand, one of the lessons of Joshua 6, especially when contrasted with the following battle against Ai, is that obedience leads to victory even over the most powerful city, while disobedience leads to defeat even against Ai, whose name means "Dump." If it didn't really happen, there is no substance to the theological/ethical point being made.

In addition, as Long points out,[4] a negative conclusion would also throw doubt on our confidence in the Scriptural record. In other words, why should we have confidence in the biblical testimony of the resurrection, if Scripture is not to be trusted in other places where it is making historical claims?

Thus, while our faith would not be definitively shattered if Jericho was not razed or the Sea did not part, it would be severely shaken.

Establishing a track record. The book of Exodus is a work of theological history. However, theological intentions do not mitigate its historical purpose. The book intends to teach us about God and his relationship with us by describing how he acted in history.

In the exodus, God acted to rescue his people from an impossible situation. Pharaoh and his chariot troops had cornered the unarmed Israelite people with their backs literally against the water. They could not go forward, backward, or sideways. There was absolutely no possible route of escape available to them. However, in response to their prayers God opened up a way through the Sea. Thus, they escaped. Further, the Egyptians followed and God used the same act to both rescue his people and judge their enemies.

The story thus teaches us a great deal about God. He is the Savior and the Judge.

Yet, if the event described by the story did not happen, it would teach us nothing about God. The story has no power apart from the event. If God did not actually rescue, why would we think of him as a Savior? If

---

[4]Long, *Art of Biblical History,* pp. 116-18.

he did not actually judge, why would we think of him as a Judge?

The account of the exodus establishes a track record for God. He is more than words. He acts on his words. Such a past action elicits present confidence and hope for the future after the event. If God could do such a marvelous act to save his people in the past, he could certainly do so in the present. This, after all, is how the Exodus tradition is used in later Scripture.

The use of the exodus in later tradition. The importance of the historical basis of the exodus account is also emphasized by its use in later biblical tradition. The exodus story echoes through Scripture, remembered in a variety of ways and for a number of different purposes. Psalm 77 illustrates one such use of the tradition:

Psalm 77. Psalm 77 is an individual lament. The psalmist begins by expressing deep emotional pain, but not specifying the cause. The latter is typical of the psalms. They almost certainly were written in the light of the poet's experience, but the specific event is suppressed so that later worshipers can use the psalm as their prayer in similar though not necessarily identical circumstances.[5]

After comparing his present distress with the bliss of the past (Ps 77:4-6), he blames God. In a series of rhetorical questions (Ps 77:7-9), he accuses God of breaking his covenant promise that he would care and protect him.

Abruptly, however, the psalmist changes his tune from accusation to praise in Psalm 77:13-15. Laments frequently demonstrate such turns, leaving the later reader wondering why. Note, for instance, the movement in Psalm 69 from verse 29 to 30:

> *I am suffering and in pain.*
>   *Rescue me, O God, by your saving power.*
> *I will praise God's name with singing,*
>   *and I will honor him with thanksgiving.*

Though no explanation for the change is stated in Psalm 69, Psalm 77

---

[5]Tremper Longman III, *How to Read the Psalms* (Downers Grove, Ill.: InterVarsity Press, 1987).

is clear about what motivates the poet to praise. It is the past and specifically it is the exodus, the crossing of the Sea. Remembrance of the past
triggers confidence in the present and hope for the future.

Verses 11-12 of Psalm 77 begin the move:

> *But then I recall all you have done, O* Lord;
> *I remember your wonderful deeds of long ago.*
> *They are constantly in my thoughts.*
> *I cannot stop thinking about your mighty works.*

And then verses 16-20 end the poem with a reflection on God's act at
the Sea.

> *When the Red Sea saw you, O God,*
> *its waters looked and trembled!*
> *The sea quaked to its very depths.*
> *The clouds poured down rain;*
> *the thunder rumbled in the sky.*
> *Your arrows of lightning flashed.*
> *Your thunder roared from the whirlwind;*
> *the lightning lit up the world!*
> *The earth trembled and shook.*
> *Your road led through the sea,*
> *your pathway through the mighty waters—*
> *a pathway no one knew was there!*
> *You led your people along that road like a flock of sheep*
> *with Moses and Aaron as their shepherds.*

Interestingly, but not uniquely (see Ps 114), the poet personifies the
waters and envisions the moment as a conflict of sorts between God and
the Sea. In this way, the poet utilizes the age-old motif of the waters
representing the forces of evil and chaos (and probably in this instance
specifically the Egyptian army, the agent of evil).

The psalmist's move from severe agitation to calm is now understandable. He is presently in the position of the Israelites at the Sea, in trouble
and beyond human aid. But God is in the business, he remembers, of
saving his people in such circumstances. When God saves when there is

no human help, then those he rescues know beyond a shadow of doubt who helped them.

Notice it is because God actually saved his people in the past that the psalmist finds confidence and hope for his present. To belabor the point, it is because God has established a track record with his people—he actually did it—that the psalmist can find relief. Imagine telling the psalmist it is a story, and in this case the often misused "it's just a story" is to the point. God never actually saved anyone. It would completely and utterly eviscerate the point of the psalmist.

Again, the point of this section is not to argue that the exodus did take place. Rather it is to point out that it loses its significance if it did not. Psalm 77 demonstrates that the power of the story of the exodus is in its connection with the event of the exodus.

DID JOB HAVE TO REALLY SUFFER FOR THE BOOK TO BE TRUE?

Does our insistence on the historical quality of the exodus event extend to the rest of the Old Testament as well? Certainly not. In this section, we will briefly examine the case of another biblical book: Job.

The book of Job sends mixed signals concerning its literary type. Likely, the genre of the book was clear to its ancient audience, but at such a historical distance, we do not have the literary sensitivity to be dogmatic.

It is unnecessary for our purposes to run through all the nuances of this issue.[6] On the side of reading the book as fiction is the presentation of the dialogue in poetic format. Poetry indicates artifice. People do not and did not speak to one another in elaborate poetic speeches like we see in Job 3:1–42:6. Granted the Bible never reports speech as if it was spoken into a microphone. While all speech is presented with artifice, the dialogues of Job go to an extreme, likely to raise the level of discourse from a specific historical event to the level of general ethical and theological reflection. Poetry elevates the book from a specific historical

---

[6]For more, see T. Longman and R. Dillard, *An Introduction to the Old Testament*, 2nd ed. (Grand Rapids: Zondervan, 2006), pp. 224-36.

event to a story with universal application. The book of Job, then, may not be a historical chronicle but rather the expression of wisdom that is to be applied to all who hear it.

On the other hand, the book begins like a historical narrative. Formally, we can detect no real grammatical difference between the opening lines of the book and books that do have historical intent (compare with the opening verses of Judges 17 and 1 Samuel 1).

A broader discussion of this issue would include comment about the mention of Job in other places in the Bible (Ezek 14:14, 20) and a comparison between Job and similar extrabiblical books (*Ludlul bel Nemeqi* and the Babylonian Theodicy).

On a full analysis, our conclusion would be that it is not certain whether we should judge Job historical or fictional or, as is probably more likely, historical fiction.

Our question, though, is does it matter? And, if not, why doesn't it matter with Job when we argued that it did matter with the exodus and the crossing of the Sea?

The theological significance of the exodus, including the crossing of the Sea, depends on its historicity, because it is an integral part of the history of redemption. A crucial feature of biblical religion is that God entered space and time to be involved with his people. He participates in history in order to rescue his people from the effects of sin. The exodus contributes to this redemptive history that leads to Christ.

On the other hand, Job's suffering does not serve a redemptive purpose. Job's pain does not alleviate our pain. Job's story rather serves a didactic purpose. It teaches us that suffering is not always the result of personal sin. Job is the ideal wise, righteous person, and yet he suffers. Thus, we cannot judge people's piety or morality based on their success or suffering.

Again, the case of Job may be contrasted with the exodus in regard to the question of theology and history. The book reminds us that we should not automatically assume that all biblical narrative must have a historical intention. On the other hand, we cannot use a book like Job to diminish the theological importance of the historical nature of the exodus event.

SUMMARY AND CONCLUSION

In the final analysis, we must concede that we cannot prove that the exodus happened to all impartial and neutral observers. This conclusion results from the fact that there is no direct evidence for the exodus event, save one.

The one text that directly provides testimony for the exodus is the book of Exodus.[7] Of course, the quality of the book of Exodus (and the whole Old Testament) is a matter of intense disagreement and debate. Those, like myself, who have confidence in the book of Exodus as a witness to actual events will be untroubled by a lack of external evidence that supports it, while those who do not share this perspective will disregard it.

Upon reflection, we should not be surprised to find ourselves in the position of affirming the historical foundation of our faith apart from external evidence that would convince every scholar. The exodus stands along with the patriarchs, the conquest, the period of the Judges, the early monarchy, even the crucifixion and resurrection itself in this regard.

We thus find ourselves in the school of Augustine, "I believe in order to understand," not in the school of Aquinas, "I understand in order to believe." But we are also not in the school of Tertullian, "I believe because it is absurd."

The archaeological evidence, which is conducive to more than one interpretation, can be read in such a way as to lend support to the view that the exodus happened.

And, finally and importantly, we cannot permit ourselves the easy way out by saying it does not matter. The exodus loses its theological and ethical significance if it did not happen in space and time.

QUESTIONS FOR DISCUSSION

1. Do you agree that the historicity of the exodus event is theologically important? Why or why not?

---

[7]For the role of testimony in historical research, see Provan, Long and Longman, *A Biblical History of Israel*, pp. 43-50.

2. Can you imagine any real, lasting value to the exodus if it did not happen?

3. In this chapter, we argued that the historicity of Job is not important to the message of that book. Do you agree or disagree? Why?

4. What other books (or parts of books) might be more like the book of Job in this regard?

FOR FURTHER READING

Long, V. P. *The Art of Biblical History*. Grand Rapids: Zondervan, 1994.

Provan, I., V. P. Long and T. Longman III. *A Biblical History of Israel*. Louisville: Westminster John Knox, 2003.

4

READING EXODUS

AS GOD'S STORY

■ ■ ■

With the background provided in the previous chapters, we now interpret the book of Exodus itself. The following is not a full-blown commentary offering a verse-by-verse or even a unit-by-unit analysis. Rather it is an orientation to what I consider to be the right approach to the book, picking up on particularly interesting highlights. It hopefully provides a framework for further and more detailed exploration of the book.

The three chapters of part four follow the outline presented in chapter two. Chapter seven explores the story of God's rescue of Israel from their bondage in Israel. Special attention will be given to the birth of Moses, his call at the burning bush, the plagues and the stirring account of the crossing of the Sea. As will be abundantly clear, these events constitute the most important story of divine rescue in the Old Testament.

In chapter eight, we will examine the Book of the Covenant (Ex 19–24). The setting is Mount Sinai, the location of Moses' earlier commission at the burning bush. Here God will meet with Israel to forge a bond with them that hereafter will be known as the Mosaic covenant. At the heart of this covenant is law, and the bulk of this section enumerates the laws that God imparted to Israel through Moses.

The third and final part of the book of Exodus (Ex 25–40) describes the construction of the tabernacle, an ornate tent in which God makes his presence known to his people. Particular attention will be paid to the symbolic value of the parts of the structure. Often allegorical interpretations have been adopted to explain the tabernacle's significance, but our close analysis will reveal a more systematic and coherent significance. In the center of this unit we hear of the episode of the Golden Calf, an event that threatens the very relationship between God and his people.

As we survey the different parts of Exodus in some detail, it is important to remember the thematic studies undertaken in chapter three. There we described important developments within the book, including (1) from the absence of God to his abiding presence as well as (2) from the malign enslavement to Egypt to the benevolent bondage to Yahweh. Further, we observed how the themes of covenant and redemption played an important role in the movement of the book.

SEVEN

GOD RESCUES ABRAHAM'S DESCENDANTS
FROM EGYPTIAN BONDAGE

(Exodus 1–18)

The departure from Egypt, the subject of the first part of the book of Exodus (Ex 1–18), has captured people's imagination from the time Israel left Egypt up to the present day. No event of the Old Testament, no act of God before the cross, has the same importance as the exodus. Within the Bible the frequent echoes to this event attest to its significance (see chapter 10). Beyond the Bible, we can point to numerous paintings and works of art, not to mention three major movies in the past century. Cecil B. DeMille made both a silent picture (1923) and a glossy color film (1956) of the exodus. More recently, Stephen Spielberg directed the animated feature *The Prince of Egypt*. Large audiences for these movies demonstrate interest in the story that goes beyond the boundaries of church and synagogue.

Even so, connected to a general apathy concerning the Old Testament, Christians may not appreciate the power and richness of the exodus. They may know about the apex of God's rescue at the Sea of Reeds, but only have general knowledge about the events leading up to that great moment. In addition, while cinematic treatment of the exodus attests to its popularity, both directors were creative in their retelling, sometimes skewing proper understanding of the story.

While it is necessary to rehearse some of the well known story line, the following exposition intends to focus on highlights and to bring out aspects of the text that may be hidden from modern readers. Such an approach involves making explicit the literary devices used by the author to tell the story. Sometimes it means describing the ancient Near Eastern background to customs. At other times, it will be important to dwell on how God chose to reveal himself to his people. Unfortunately, it also means debunking some popular misconceptions.

The story begins during the reign of an unnamed Pharaoh who "knew nothing about Joseph or what he had done" (Ex 1:8).

A PHARAOH WHO DID NOT KNOW JOSEPH (EXODUS 1:1-22)

Genesis ended with an account of the death of Joseph (Gen 50:22-26), thus providing some sense of closure to the story of his life and to the book as a whole. However, just before his death, Joseph is recorded as saying: "God will surely come to help you and lead you out of this land of Egypt. He will give you back to the land he solemnly promised to give to Abraham, to Isaac, and to Jacob. . . . When God comes to help you and lead you back, you must take my bones with you" (Gen 50:24-25). Clearly, these words hint strongly at a sequel and that sequel is the book of Exodus.

Exodus, after all, is chapter (or perhaps, volume) two of a larger literary work, the five-part Torah. Genesis serves as a preface to the last four books, Exodus through Deuteronomy, which tell the story of Moses, covering the time period from his birth to his death. But in the final analysis, this is not Moses' story, it is the story of God's fulfilling his promises to Abraham and taking his people and making them a "great nation" by bringing them out of captivity and into the Promised Land (see Gen 12:1-3).

Indeed, it is a part, a dramatic part to be sure, of God's plan to bring blessing to his human creatures. Genesis told the story of the creation of Adam and Eve, placing them in the Garden of Eden where he "blessed them." However, Genesis 3 told the story of the loss of blessing due to Adam and Eve's rebellion, their assertion of moral autonomy by eating the fruit of the prohibited tree. They were thus ejected from Eden.

In spite of their sin, God determined to pursue his human creatures, desiring to restore his relationship with them and bestowing his blessing on them once again. A tremendous transition takes place in Genesis 12, when God determines to bring blessing to the nations through the choice of one man, Abraham, who would be the father of a nation and that nation would be a conduit of the blessing of God to all the nations.

Thus it is that Joseph at the end of his life knows that his descendants will not remain forever in Egypt. Their future is in the Promised Land. Even Joseph himself would end up in the promised land when his embalmed body was buried there at the end of Joshua's conquest of the land (Josh 24:32, after having been taken there by Moses [Ex 13:19]).

The book of Exodus accordingly begins with a hook that reminds us of the beginnings of Israel in Egypt, the seventy (textual variant has seventy-five, see also Gen 46:27) members of the family of God who had gone down to Egypt to survive a devastating famine and ended up staying.

The action of Exodus starts some centuries, we cannot tell precisely how many, after the death of Joseph. There are some questions about the date of Joseph and even more about the date of the exodus (see chapter 5), but it was long enough that the family of God had grown to nation size.

When Genesis ended, the Pharaoh, also unnamed there, was extremely fond of Joseph. After all, though a hated Asiatic, Joseph had hit on a formula that enriched and empowered Pharaoh beyond imagination. But now a Pharaoh had arisen that did not know Joseph and therefore he was afraid of Joseph's descendants. They were, after all, a potential foreign enemy within the boundaries of Egypt.

Some speculation points to Ahmose (c. 1550–1525 B.C.) as the Pharaoh who did not know (that is appreciate) Joseph. His antipathy for Asiatic people, of which the Israelites would be an example, was well founded in the Hyksos invasion of Egypt. The Hyksos were Asiatic people who invaded Egypt and ruled it for at least a hundred years at the end of the so-called Second Intermediate Period (1720–1550 B.C.), a period of great social turmoil.[1] It was Ahmose, a native Egyptian, who finally expelled these hated occupiers. No wonder he would cast a suspicious eye on the children of Israel, who were the Hyksos' ethnic cousins.

Thus was initiated a new phase of Egyptian-Israelite relationships characterized by enslavement and the mandate to kill all male babies. The Israelites were charged to perform heavy labor, building the cities of Pithom and Rameses. The destruction of male babies was the responsibility of the two midwives, Shiphrah and Puah. While identified as "midwives of the Hebrews," some in the history of interpretation have thought they were Egyptians (and thus righteous Gentiles, see Septuagint; Josephus), while others take the more likely approach that they themselves were Hebrew (the Talmud, which also identifies them as Jochebed and Miriam).[2] That there were two indicates either that they were the head midwives or, as probably is more likely, there were not as many Israelites as popularly imagined.

The midwives lied by saying their failure to perfectly execute their orders was the result of the hardiness of Israelite women. Thus initiates a theme of deception in the telling of the exodus that has generated much discussion as an ethical problem. The text itself never condemns their lie, though the Hebrew narrator is famously reticent with moral judgments. Calvin, for instance, believed they sinned, though God extended his grace to them and forgave them.[3] However, rather than thinking there is an implicit condemnation here, it is more likely that Shiphrah and Puah are thought to be doing the right thing. After all, the Pharaoh forfeited his right to the truth by his murderous intentions toward Israelite baby boys.

It is on this background of enslavement, exploitation, and mass murder that we hear the account of Moses' birth.

---

[1]See N. Sarna, *Exploring Exodus: The Origins of Biblical Israel,* 2nd ed. (New York: Schocken, 1996), pp. 15-16.
[2]S. M. Langston, *Exodus Through the Centuries* (Oxford: Blackwell, 2006), p. 18.
[3]Ibid., p. 20.

RESCUE FROM THE WATER: MOSES' BIRTH STORY (EXODUS 2:1-10)

The story of Moses' birth begins with the introduction of his parents. No names are given, but we learn right away of their tribal affiliation. They are Levites. Of course, at this point of the story we only know that Levites are a disenfranchised tribe. They are nothing special, except exceptionally cursed. Due to the vengeful acts of Levi (Gen 34), Jacob, his father, cursed him and his brother Simeon. He, in essence, disinherited them both from receiving a tribal allotment once their descendants entered the land (Gen 49:5-7). As we will later see, the story of the Levites is far from over (see chapter 8). When the book of Exodus was likely written and certainly when most readers encounter it, the Levites *are* a special tribe, a priestly tribe, thus the emphasis is on Moses' (and Aaron's) tribal connection. Indeed, the association with the Levites is so strong that the narrative at this point does not tell us their names. Later, beginning with Exodus 6:3, we learn that Moses' father is Amram and Moses' mother is Jochebed.

The previous section informed the reader that the Pharaoh had ordered the death of male babies born to Hebrews. The midwives though were always "late" getting to the births and so it apparently was for Jochebed. She had time to try to save her baby's life. What she did seems like a desperate act, a shot in the dark almost. However, it only appears that way to the modern reader. Her actions are calculated and show a tremendous trust in God. She took her baby and put him in a papyrus basket and placed him on the Nile.

As we observed in chapter four, our understanding of her actions is enriched by the discovery of another birth story, that of Sargon (the Great), an Akkadian king who ruled at the end of the third millennium B.C. (see discussion in chapter 4). This account is known today as the Sargon Birth Legend, and though the story is about the Akkadian Sargon, it is likely that it was written during the reign of a later Assyrian king who took on the name Sargon and who ruled in the last part of the eighth century B.C.[4] Sargon was born to a high priestess. We are not told

---

[4]For a translation and more information about this text, see Tremper Longman III, *Fictional Akkadian Autobiography* (Winona Lake, Ind.: Eisenbrauns, 1991), pp. 53-60, 215-16.

why she needs to hide the fact that she has had a child, but it may have something to do with her position. In any case, she can't keep baby Sargon, but she also does not want to dispose of him in the typical way of exposure. Thus, she prepares a "reed basket" and floats him down the Euphrates. An irrigation digger discovers the basket and raises him. From that lowly position, he rises to become the first builder of an empire in southern Mesopotamia.

Moses' story is the reverse, at least from a socio-economic perspective. His mother was a slave, the one who discovered him and raised him was none other than the daughter of the Pharaoh who wanted all Hebrew boys killed, a truly ironic reversal. The very child that Pharaoh's murderous policies were shaped to kill actually grew up in his very house.

The discovery of the Sargon Birth Legend at the end of the nineteenth century has been interpreted in different ways.[5] When first translated by George Smith at the British Museum, he thought he uncovered the origins of the "myth" of Moses' birth. Just as likely, even more likely, he uncovered an ancient strategy for mothers who had to give up their baby even though they wanted to keep it. In a word, both Sargon's mother and Jochebed committed their baby's to the care of their God. Jochebed hoped that God would save her child from death, and he did. Even more than that, he created the conditions for her to actually be the wet nurse for baby Moses (Ex 2:7-8). She even got paid!

As strange as this story sounds to modern ears, it was not strange to ancient Near Eastern ones. In addition, the story fits in with a well-known theme in the Old Testament. True, this story is unique in the Bible. No other baby survives birth in quite the same way. But countless stories describe births to mothers who were previously barren. Sarah, Rebekah, Rachel, Hannah, Samson's unnamed mother—all were barren, but God opened their womb. Why so many troubled births? In this way, God makes it clear that these children, including Moses, are special gifts of God. These are the ones who either continue the line of

---

[5]See B. Lewis, *The Sargon Birth Legend: A Study of the Akkadian Text and the Tale of the Hero Who Was Exposed at Birth* (Cambridge: American Schools of Oriental Research, 1980).

promise or save God's people from destruction. It is against this background, as a matter of fact, that we should understand the significance of Jesus' virgin birth. It is not just a "signs and wonders" show. The virgin birth makes an important theological statement. If Isaac and Moses, among other Old Testament characters, are shown in this way to be gifts of God by virtue of their birth to previously barren women, how much more so Jesus, born from a virgin's womb.

THE BURNING BUSH AND THE RETURN TO EGYPT (EXODUS 3:1–4:31)

Few biblical moments are as widely known as the episode at the burning bush. To invoke the image calls to mind an intense encounter with God. Not only did Moses enter the presence of God at the bush, he also received his life-changing commission to return to Egypt and lead the Israelites out of enslavement.

But what brought him to the burning bush? We learn precious little about Moses in Egypt after his birth. Jewish legends (for instance, one found in Josephus, the first century A.D. writer) and modern movies may well be right that he received an education and a position befitting a son of Pharaoh, but we hear nothing about it in the narrative. The next story we hear in the biblical text concerns Moses coming to the aid of a Hebrew slave being beaten by an Egyptian overlord. Moses kills the Egyptian, and whatever position he had before Pharaoh evaporated quickly since he had to flee the country. Moses sought refuge in Midian, a region of no definite boundaries at this time, since the Midianites were a nomadic people, but the area is to be associated with the Sinai Peninsula as well as the area to the east of the Gulf of Aqaba.

Upon reaching Midian, he rescued some women in distress at a well. The setting at a well raises the reader's expectations. After all, in Genesis we first encounter Rebekah at a well (Gen 24:15-17), as well as Rachel (Gen 29:1-14), with accounts of their marriages to Isaac and Jacob soon recounted.[6] Moses also soon married one of the rescued women, Zip-

---

[6]Robert Alter, *The Art of Biblical Narrative* (New York: Basic Books, 1981), calls this a type-scene, defined as "certain fixed situations which the poet is expected to include in

porah, daughter of Jethro, and he became one of the family and a shep-
herd like the others.

The moment of truth comes a number of years later at the burning
bush (Ex 3:1–4:23). Why did God appear to Moses? He determined to
save his people because "he remembered his covenant promise to Abraham, Isaac, and Jacob" (Ex 2:24). Now was the time to act, he knew,
because his people cried to him for help.

But why did God make his presence known to Moses in the form of a
burning bush? While the burning bush was a unique expression of
God's appearance, it included components of earlier theophanies (the
technical term for an appearance of God).

In the first place, trees and objects related to trees (rods and in this
case a bush) are often found in places made sacred by God's presence. Of
course, trees represent life and God is the author of life. Trees are at the
center of Eden and thus holy places are often marked by a tree (Gen
12:6; 13:18) or a symbolic tree like the menorah (see tree-like description at Ex 25:31-40). In the second place, fire, often accompanied by
smoke, also represents God's presence. In Genesis 15:17, God walked
through the divided animals in the form of a "firepot and a flaming
torch." At a later time, smoke and fire could be seen on the top of Mount
Sinai when God appeared to Moses again to give him the Ten Commandments (Ex 19:18). During the wilderness wandering, the Israelites
were led by a pillar of smoke by day and a pillar of fire by night.

Fire and smoke draw attention. One's gaze cannot penetrate beyond
fire or smoke, so they both represent God's holy presence, but hide him
from human sight. Fire is an agent of cleansing and refinement as well.
Fire can warm but also destroy. It is a powerful image of God's presence.
Gowan describes the effect of the immediate presence of God with
words that are also appropriate for fire. They are both "frightening and
attractive, daunting and fascinating."[7]

And here we have a bush that does not burn, a sight that certainly

---

his narrative and which he must perform according to a set order of motifs" (p. 50).

[7]D. E. Gowan, *Theology in Exodus: Biblical Theology in the Form of a Commentary* (Philadelphia: Westminster John Knox, 1994), p. 28.

draws one's attention, and it captured Moses'. Such a thing cannot happen—unless God makes it happen. Rationalist attempts to explain the burning bush as the spontaneous igniting of natural gas coming up out of a crack in the ground or a volcanic vent simply cater to modern sensibilities.[8] We should understand this phenomenon as Moses surely did, a miracle that demonstrated God's presence at a crucial time.

At the bush, God commissions Moses to return to Egypt and lead the people out of bondage. Moses hesitates, first out of a sense of inadequacy, "Who am I to appear before Pharaoh? Who am I to lead the people out of Egypt?" (Ex 3:11). In response, God does not point to Moses' status or skill. He simply says, "I will be with you." This phrase is a shorthand reminder of God's covenant promise. The phrase occurs frequently in the narratives of Genesis. As one example, notice how often the phrase is stated in Genesis 39 (see Gen 39:2, 3, 23) while Joseph is in Potiphar's house. It is the explanation for his tremendous success in the chapter.

Moses, however, is not moved to obedience. He continues to protest, this time that he does not have God's name. Admittedly, the interchange between God and Moses is hard to figure out in detail. Certain things are clear and others are not. For instance, is this the first occasion that the divine name Yahweh has been uttered? If so, there are a couple of problems. One is that Genesis uses the name Yahweh. Of course, this may be a later retrojection of the name into an earlier time and Wenham has pointed out that the divine name is most frequently found in the narrative, not in the dialogue.[9] Perhaps even more puzzling is how the revelation of the name will help Moses when he actually appears to the people in Egypt. If God has not been known by the name Yahweh, why would this assure the people that Moses was a bonafide representative of the God they knew as the "God of Abraham, Isaac and Jacob"?

Some questions we just can't answer. But we can explore further the

---

[8]See Colin Humphreys, *The Miracles of Exodus: A Scientist's Discovery of the Extraordinary Natural Causes of the Biblical Stories* (San Francisco: HarperSanFrancisco, 2003), pp. 61-81.

[9]Gordon J. Wenham, "The Religion of the Patriarchs," in *Essays on the Patriarchal Narratives*, ed. A. R. Millard and D. J. Wiseman (Winona Lake, Ind.: Eisenbrauns, 1983), pp. 157-88.

significance of the name. In the first place, it is a personal name. There are many gods *(elohim),* but there is only one Yahweh, just like there are many humans, but just one Tremper Longman III.

Second, in antiquity, especially in the Bible, names have significant meanings. The name Yahweh is connected to a Hebrew verb *haya,* "to be." It is the verb of existence. God himself explains the significance of his name when he says, "I Am Who I Am." In other words, God claims that he is self-defining. He is unable to be narrowed down. He is the ground of existence. It is an awesome name, a name that he reveals to his covenant partners.

Moses still hesitates. Perhaps he wonders too why the revelation of the name would give him any cachet with the people. God does not complain. He gives him signs to perform. Later we will learn that prophets, to be believed, must have signs that confirm their status (Deut 18:15-22). Moses will be able to throw down his rod and it will turn into a serpent. We have already observed above that a rod, as in essence a mobile tree, can represent God's presence. We will comment on the significance of the rod turning into a serpent later. As a second sign, Moses can put his hand inside his cloak and it will turn leprous. He can then repeat the action and his skin will become clean again.

Even so, Moses remains hesitant, this time complaining he is not a good speaker. Finally, God grows angry with Moses. Even so, rather than forcing him to act as his only spokesman, he recruits Aaron to join him. Interestingly, while Moses is a prophet for God, now Aaron is a prophet for Moses (Ex 4:15-17).

Satisfied that Aaron will accompany him, Moses takes leave of Jethro and begins the journey to Egypt. On the way, in what is certainly one of the most unexpected and bizarre stories in redemptive history, God attacked Moses, his servant. The text states that God was going to kill "him." The pronoun has an ambiguous antecedent, but most likely "him" refers to Moses, not his son. In either case, the measure God takes is extreme and much about this story remains enigmatic. Zipporah acts quickly and angrily to save her family by performing a circumcision on her son. Thus, one thing about this story is crystal clear. It illustrates the importance of circumcision. It is a matter of life and death.

THE PLAGUES: THE WAR AGAINST
THE GODS OF EGYPT (EXODUS 5:1–11:9)

In this section, we will not give a detailed blow-by-blow description of the plagues. Rather we will raise certain major themes and deal with important and difficult issues in order to gain an appropriate perspective by which to read and understand this section of the book of Exodus.

Moses' request to take a three-day journey. God sent Moses in response to the cry of the people for help due to the extreme conditions of their bondage (Ex 2:23-25). On the basis of the covenant he made with Abraham, God determined to deliver them from their bondage. Even more, he wanted Moses to lead them to "a land flowing with milk and honey—the land where the Canaanites, Hittites, Amorites, Perizzites, Hivites, and Jebusites now live" (Ex 3:8). Right from the start, it appears, God's intention was to effect a permanent liberation from Egypt.

Why then does God tell Moses to confront Pharaoh and ask for a "three-day journey into the wilderness to offer sacrifices to the LORD, our God" (Ex 3:18), which he does upon arrival in Egypt (Ex 5:3)? In other words, it appears that God commanded Moses to dissimulate, indeed lie, to Pharaoh. He asks for three days, but if granted, it seems that there is no doubt but that the Israelites would keep going. Indeed, when Pharaoh finally does give permission to Moses, it is unclear whether or not he thinks that the Israelites are just going for three days (Ex 3:18; 5:3; 8:27).

The whole issue of what constitutes a lie is more complex than it seems at first glance. The ninth commandment clearly states "You shall not give false testimony against your neighbor" (Ex 20:16). While it is true that the specific language of the commandment situates it within the courtroom, it seems special pleading to think that God did not care about deception outside of the justice system. True, the commandment interestingly prohibits false testimony against a neighbor, and "an act of deception against a fellow member of the Israelite community is never described in favorable or even acceptable terms."[10] Are the Egyptians

---

[10]M. J. Williams, *Deception in Genesis: An Investigation into the Morality of a Unique Biblical Phenomenon* (New York: Peter Lang, 2001), p. 64.

not considered a neighbor? Perhaps not. After all, we have already seen that the midwives lied in order to save the lives of newborn children. Here lying is once again in the service of saving lives. Again, we should consider the Pharaoh as a person who has forfeited the right to the truth since he would use the truth to further unjustly oppress the Israelites.

Pharaoh's hard heart. Readers of Exodus stumble over the book's language about God hardening Pharaoh's heart. Indeed, in Exodus 4:21 God announced his intention to Moses, "When you arrive back in Egypt, go to Pharaoh and perform all the miracles I have empowered you to do. But I will harden his heart so he will refuse to let the people go." And indeed, that is precisely what happens (see Ex 7:3; 9:12; 10:1, 20, 27; 11:10, as well as the description of Pharaoh's condition in Ex 7:13, 22; 8:19; 9:35). Even after the Pharaoh allows Israel to leave Egypt, God will harden his heart and indeed the hearts of all the Egyptians (Ex 14:7-8, 17), so he and they change their mind and pursue them at the Sea of Reeds.

It all seems so unfair, as if God is setting the Pharaoh up for destruction. Interestingly, however, there is another theme running through the plague sections of Exodus, the theme that Pharaoh hardened his own heart (Ex 8:15, 32; 9:34). So it appears that both God and Pharaoh hardened his heart. What does this mean? Much remains mysterious, but one thing is certain. God did not make Pharaoh mean, evil and stubborn. He may well have intensified it or at least he did not soften Pharaoh's heart.

But why not? Why wouldn't God simply soften his heart so he felt compassion toward the Israelites and allowed them to go? Again, the Bible does not come out and make a cause-and-effect statement, but we do know that Pharaoh's stubbornness meant that the plagues grew in intensity and led eventually to the dramatic moment on the shores of the Sea of Reeds. In this way, God both displayed his glorious power and he brought judgment on Pharaoh, the Egyptian people and even, as we will see below, the Egyptian gods.[11]

---

[11]So Sarna, *Exploring Exodus*, p. 65, "In brief, the idea of God's hardening the pharaoh's heart is that He utilizes a man's natural proclivity toward evil; He accentuates the pro-

The plagues as a victory over the gods of Egypt. Just before the final and back-breaking plague of the death of the firstborn, God announces: "On that night I will pass through the land of Egypt and strike down every firstborn son and firstborn male animal in the land of Egypt. I will execute judgment against all the gods of Egypt, for I am the LORD!" (Ex 12:12). This thought is repeated in Numbers 33:4: "The LORD had defeated the gods of Egypt that night with great acts of judgment!"

In these pronouncements we witness an essential aspect of the plagues that readers often miss. They are not just plagues against Egypt, or even plagues against Pharaoh alone, they are attacks on the Egyptian gods.

The first question that arises has to do with the existence of the gods of Egypt. After all, isn't there one and only one God, the true God of Israel—Yahweh? The answer to that question is much more complex than one might think.

In perhaps the most important sense, the answer is yes. There is only one God who created all other things and beings. This answer must be nuanced though in the light of the biblical teaching and understanding that other gods also exist. Besides the above quoted passages, we might think of Psalm 82 that speaks of God's judgment on the gods. We might also consider Deuteronomy 32:8. Here later scribes, probably worried that the important biblical concept of monotheism might be compromised, changed the text at a critical point, but scholars are convinced, based on the powerful textual witness of the Septuagint backed by scrolls from the Dead Sea, that the passage should read:

> When the Most High assigned lands to the nations,
>   when he divided up the human race,
> he established the boundaries of the peoples
>   according to the number of the sons of God.

The phrase "sons of God" is a common way to refer to the "gods" in the Old Testament and in surrounding cultures like that represented by the Ugarit materials.

---

cess in furtherance of His own historical purposes."

The point isn't that there are beings equal to Yahweh but that there are spiritual beings with power, created by God to be sure and assigned their place by God (according to Deuteronomy 32), but who are spiritual entities and are known as gods. The Egyptian gods are such spiritual powers. A later time will call them angels or spiritual powers. That such spiritual powers are associated with nation states may be seen in Daniel 10, where Gabriel tells Daniel that the spirit prince of Persia had delayed his coming. The gods of Egypt were like the spirit prince of Persia, powerful and resistant to the will of God. Other spirit princes, like Michael the spirit prince of Israel, have remained faithful to God. There is, in other words, a spiritual battle that goes on behind the human conflicts that we can see with our eyes.

The plagues were attacks on these gods. That these gods had some power may be seen in the fact that the Egyptian magicians, servants of these spirit princes, can mimic the early actions of Moses and Aaron. After Moses and Aaron's staffs transform into serpents, they can throw down their staffs and they too become serpents (Ex 7:1-13). But even here God is shown to be superior by virtue of the fact that the Israelites' serpents swallow those of the Egyptians. The Egyptian gods can take it to the next level when the magicians again are able to mimic Moses and Aaron by turning water into blood. Even with the next plague, the plague of frogs, the magicians can cause frogs to come up from the Nile River.

But right after these three early signs of God's power, the Egyptian gods are left far behind. God then pounds away at Egypt until they finally agree to release the Israelites from bondage.

Some scholars want to go further than simply asserting that the plagues are battles against the "gods of Egypt." They insist that the individual plagues are tailored against a specific deity. At times, this approach makes sense. For instance, the Nile River was the source of all the agricultural fertility in the land. If there were no Nile, there would be no Egypt. The god of fertility, Hapi, was accordingly closely related to the Nile River. One can see the rationale behind the belief that when the Nile was attacked by turning its waters into blood that that would be envisioned as an attack on Hapi. Certainly, the ninth plague, the plague that plunged most of Egypt into darkness, would be seen as an attack on the all-important sun god (who went by various names and manifestations, including Amon and Re). Each day Re was thought to travel the celestial sea in his boat, then descend into the netherworld where he defeated the serpent of chaos, Apophis, to arise anew and victorious every morning. For the world to plunge into darkness would mean that Re had been defeated. The last plague, the death of the firstborn, would be an attack on the household of Pharaoh himself.

While this approach makes some sense, it begins to unravel as the other plagues are connected to specific gods. One example is the attempt to talk about the theological background of the plague of frogs. The best that can be done with this plague is to connect it to a god who was often pictured with a frog's head.

While not trying to press the details in this way, the main point stands clearly and powerfully. The successful plagues represented a putting of the Egyptian "gods" in their place.

Are the plagues extraordinary but natural events? Many have tried to understand the plagues not as miracles per se, but more like extraordinary providence, that is, as involving an unusual confluence and timing of natural events. While Greta Hort[12] is the biblical scholar best known in recent times to advance such a view, more recently the British scientist Colin Humphreys[13] has written an entire book on the miracles of the exodus, a large part of which is devoted to the plagues. We will use his work to explore the viability of such an idea.

He begins with an analysis of the plague that strikes the Nile turning the river into blood. Humphreys cites a not uncommon phenomenon at the Nile, called "red tide," that is the result of "algal blooms." He believes that an unusually intense red tide happened in response to Moses' actions. He is not denying the divine connection here, just the means that God used. He does not address the question that the Bible says that God turned the Nile into blood, not that he made it look like blood.

---

[12]G. Hort, "The Plagues of Egypt," *Zeitschrift für die Alttestamentliche Wissenschaft* 69 (1957): 84-103, and 70 (1958): 48-59.

[13]C. Humphreys, *The Miracles of Exodus*, esp. pp. 111-49.

This first plague then caused the second plague, the plague of frogs. Since frogs could not stand the algae polluted river, they hopped out en masse and died from dehydration. Without frogs around to eat them, the gnats (which he identifies with *Culicoides*, midges) and flies (he says they are stable flies), the third and fourth plagues, were free to multiply and swarm around the frog carcasses. Again, Humphreys does not address the question that the text says that the gnats were produced from the dust that came from Moses' staff as it hit the ground (Ex 8:19). The death of the livestock, the fifth plague, was due to African horse sickness and bluetongue that the midges carried.

Humphreys is not absolutely certain about the cause of the boils, which the Bible associates with soot that Moses throws into the air, but he says it could be glanders or skin anthrax. Whatever it was, he argues, it was spread by the stable flies of plague four.

Thus, plagues one through six are caused by the previous plagues set off initially by the algae pollution of the Nile. The seventh plague is the plague of hail. Humphreys here cites the fact that locusts need wet soil in which to place their eggs, the wetness was therefore created by the hailstorm.

No causal connection can be drawn with the next plague of darkness. Humphreys though still posits a natural cause for the darkening of the sun, a khamsin or dust storm. Though not connected with the immediately previous plague, he does think that the flooding that he associates with the first plague left a much larger than normal amount of dirt on the ground that would have produced the large dust storm.

Hort and most naturalistic interpreters take the final, climactic plague of the firstborn as a true miracle with no causal connections with the events of the past few months. Humphreys again shows himself the most consistent in this regard by providing such an explanation. In a summary statement, he suggests that the firstborn males died from "mycotoxins on grain, possibly *macrocylic tricothecenes*. Due to damp grain from hail contaminated by locusts' feces and stored in a grain store then sealed by sand from the *khamsin* dust storm."[14] But why the first-

---

[14]Ibid., p. 145.

born males? Here Humphreys becomes exceedingly ingenious. He believes that since the future of the Egyptian family was with the firstborn male, that they would be the ones who would be privileged to eat the grain first. The dust storm would have meant that the Egyptians would not have eaten in a while, so they get there first, eat, and die in a way that warns off the rest of the population.

Humphreys has truly given the best possible presentation of the naturalistic explanation of the plagues. Indeed, his book offers similar types of explanations to all the events surrounding the exodus. In other places in this book, we will show our appreciation and acceptance of a few of his ideas. One also needs to appreciate the fact that he does not present this interpretation in order to undermine faith or distance God from what happened. Far from it, he believes that the divine miracle is that God was behind all these events and that this can be seen in the timing of events most readily. In addition, we concur that God does use secondary causes. As a matter of fact, as he points out and as is clear from the text, the splitting of the *Yam Suf* is connected to an extremely strong wind.

However, in the final analysis, I find the naturalistic explanation difficult to accept. For one thing, as I have tried to point out from time to time in the above description, the Bible itself attributes the cause of some of the plagues clearly to other than naturalistic factors (Moses striking the ground with his rod) and the descriptions of the plagues themselves do not suggest a naturalistic interpretation (the Nile became blood; it did not look like blood). Indeed, the fact that the Bible is not reticent about mentioning a naturalistic cause should provide pause into our believing there was one.

In any case, the final plague overwhelmed Pharaoh and the Egyptians. They are now ready to allow Israel to leave their bondage and depart Egypt. We now come to the Exodus itself.

THE PASSOVER AND EXODUS (EXODUS 12)

Exodus 11 anticipates and describes the final and most devastating plague, the death of the firstborn, as a future event. The historical report of the plague itself occurs in the next chapter. However, the form of the report is surprising. In the first place, it is short and to the point (Ex 12:28-30). These verses simply inform the reader that the LORD killed the firstborn of all Egyptians without exception, from the lowest echelon of society to the son of Pharaoh himself. It also mentioned that the firstborn of the animals died as well as humans and that this was a tragedy that saddened every Egyptian household.

What surprises us are the verses leading up to this point (Ex 12:1-27). It has the form of liturgical instructions. God here establishes a new annual ceremony. The Israelites were to act out the ritual on the night of the actual plague and then repeat it every year from then on. As a matter of fact, this event was so momentous that it changed the Israelite calendar. From this time on, "this month will be the first month of the year for you" (Ex 12:2), though the celebration was to begin on the tenth day of the month (Ex 12:3).

The ritual, celebrated by all Israelites, was family-based. No priests are involved; indeed, at this time, there are no Israelite priests. The commemoration centered on a lamb (or goat). The fact that the sheep (or goat) must be "a one-year-old male, either a sheep or a goat with no defects" and the fact that all its meat must be eaten or burned signal that the slaughter of the animal has sacrificial value.

The slaughter took place on the fourteenth day of the month; its blood was then smeared on the sides and top of the doorframes of the house. Likely the blood indicated that a death had already occurred in the house and therefore the angel of the LORD would pass by that house. Again, the sacrificial nature of the lamb and the atoning value of the blood is highlighted by this, the lamb acting like a substitute for those who lived in the house.[15]

The family then ate the lamb, along with "bitter salad green and bread made without yeast" (Ex 12:8). While little is made of the "bitter salad green" (traditionally "bitter herbs") of the meal, one can speculate that

---

[15]Sarna, *Exploring Exodus*, pp. 92-3, points out the irony of the fact that the exodus story begins with Pharaoh wanting to shed Israelite blood and here blood protects Israelite lives while Egyptians were dying.

the vegetable is bitter in order to symbolize that the day is filled with death. An alternative explanation is that it represents the hard, bitter work of the Israelites as they sojourned in Egypt.

The greater emphasis is on the lack of yeast in the bread. While dire and repeated warnings are issued against yeast in the bread, no reason is given. The fact that the Israelites were to dress in a way that indicates an urgent and sudden departure (Ex 12:11) may demonstrate that there was no time to allow the bread to rise.

The Passover festival thus became an annual event that reminded and reenacted the departure (exodus) from Egypt. It has been celebrated by faithful Jews to the present day. Exodus and Passover go hand in hand, an association that the New Testament writers exploit in ways to be uncovered in a later chapter (chapter 9).

THE CROSSING OF THE *YAM SUF*

Thus, the Israelites were freed from Egyptian slavery. Or were they?

As often happens in biblical narrative, just when the reader thinks the story is over, it reaches a new intensity.[16] An embarrassed and angry Pharaoh decides to pursue the departing Israelites and traps them at the *Yam Suf.*

Yam Suf is often translated Red Sea, a tradition that goes back at least to the Septuagint. However, as has often been pointed out, *Yam Suf* literally means "Sea of Reeds," and reeds do not grow in salt water like that of the Red Sea. It appears more likely that the *Yam Suf* refers to a fresh water lake that existed just north of the Gulf of Suez.[17] Some scholars have used this datum to argue that the lake was shallow and that a providential wind blew it back just far enough to allow the Israelites to wade through to safety. Granted that God did use wind as a secondary cause to push the waters back, such an explanation does not appreciate

---

[16]For example, one might think that the Abraham story reaches closure with the birth of the long-awaited promised seed, Isaac (Gen 21:1-7). However, in the very next chapter, the plot reaches a new crisis point with God's command to take Isaac and sacrifice him (see Longman, *How to Read Genesis*, pp. 134-35).

[17]See J. K. Hoffmeier, *Israel in Egypt: The Evidence for the Authenticity of the Exodus Tradition* (Oxford: Oxford University Press, 1997), pp. 203-15.

the tenor of the biblical story that describes the event as out of the ordinary. Thus, the crossing takes place at a lake that would be impassable without divine intervention. In the rest of the book, we will simply refer to this body of water as the Sea.

When he caught up with the Israelites, Pharaoh surely thought that he had them trapped. The reality of the situation was the exact opposite. God had the Egyptians trapped. God had instructed Moses to move the Israelites to a camp site on the shore of the Sea in anticipation of Pharaoh's pursuit (Ex 14:1-4). He commanded them to do so in order to display his glory.

With Pharaoh's approach, the people, who were not in on the divine plan, panicked. Moses reassured them, telling them that God would fight for them (Ex 14:14). Thus that night, he raised the walking staff, representing the presence of God over his head, and the Sea parted, allowing the Israelites to escape to the other side. The Egyptians followed, though when they were in the midst of the dry seabed God confused them so they were bogged down, permitting the Israelites to reach the other side. And once there, Moses raised his walking staff one more time and the path through the Sea disappeared, decimating the Egyptian army.

In the aftermath, Moses led the people of God in a song of celebration (Ex 15). In it, they praised the God who fought for them. In addition, they anticipated future glory as they would enter the Promised Land and settle there.

THE BEGINNINGS OF THE WILDERNESS WANDERINGS (EXODUS 15:22–18:27)

Past the Sea, Israel began its journey toward the Promised Land. The event that would doom them to forty years in the wilderness was still in the future (Num 13–14), but the people immediately demonstrated the character that would lead to that sorry moment.

We can understand how their confidence might be tried since they traveled for three days without finding water. Even when they found water, they discovered that it was undrinkable (thus giving the place its name, Marah, or "Bitter"). On the other hand, they had just experienced

God's powerful presence at the Sea. Certainly, they could muster enough trust in God to believe that he would provide them with water. Sadly, they did not. God, however, came through by instructing Moses to throw a piece of wood into the water that purified it.

Still, this episode is just the first of the complaints in the wilderness. Even before they get to Sinai, a period of only two months, we hear the Israelites grumble on a number of occasions.

In the wilderness of Sin, they complain about a lack of food. God responds by providing manna, the name deriving from the fact that the Israelites greeted God's provision with a less-than-enthusiastic response, since in Hebrew "manna" means "What is it?" God also gave the people quail.

Still, when they were thirsty again, they did not remember God's former action, but complain again. This time God instructs Moses to strike a rock with his rod with the result that the rock gushed with water. This episode prepares for a later time when Moses does not follow God's instructions closely, to his own detriment (Num 20).

While the people show their tendency toward doubt and disobedience, the leadership, particularly Moses, demonstrate their faithfulness. When Israel was attacked by the fearsome Amalekites, Moses raised his rod that symbolically indicated God's presence, and they beat back the threat.

The concluding section of this part of Exodus sees Moses back reunited with his family. Jethro, his father-in-law, provided Moses with good advice about how to deal with the overwhelming responsibilities that now occupied him. Finally, Moses leads the Israelites in the final push that brings them to the foot of Mount Sinai.

THE POPULATION OF ISRAEL AND THEIR ROUTE THROUGH THE WILDERNESS

As we consider Israel leaving Egypt and heading toward the Promised Land, two issues arise, the number of people wandering through the wilderness and the direction in which they traveled.

At the beginning of the book of Exodus, the narrator tells us that the "Israelites were fruitful and multiplied greatly and became exceedingly numerous, so that the land was filled with them" (Ex 1:7). Pharaoh's concern that they "have become too numerous for us" (Ex 1:9) indicates a significant population, but we would be hard pressed to put even an approximate number on this since we have no definite idea of the population of Egypt at this time. However, at the time of the departure from Egypt we are told that "there were about 600,000 men plus all the women and children. A rabble of non-Israelites went with them" (Ex 12:37-38). Consideration must also be given to the so-called census report of Numbers 2.[18] The total number of males from the twelve tribes that were included (Levites were not) numbered 603,550 (Num 2:32). Such a number would lead to the conclusion that there were approximately two million people involved in the exodus and wilderness wandering.

Many people balk at such a high number. How could they march through the wilderness with such a large group of people? The typical answer to this objection is that God provided for them miraculously.[19] But then why are there no remnants of their forty years in the wilderness? One would expect such a large group to leave their mark on the landscape. Again, there is a response. They are not a settled people, but nomads; one would not expect them to have or use objects that would last until the present day.

These questions and answers have their strengths and weaknesses, but before settling into hard and fast viewpoints on this matter, it must be recognized that there is some indication within the text itself that the number is far too high. In a recent article, C. J. Humphreys, the man whose naturalistic explanation of the plagues I have rejected, has pointed out that the number 603,550 is in fact inconsistent with other numbers in the text, most clearly Numbers 3:46 which says that there

---

[18]Really a military registration since it numbers males twenty years old and older.

[19]Though attempts have been made to suggest that such population growth would not be that extraordinary. See Sarna, *Exploring Exodus*, pp. 94-102. Sarna himself ultimately concludes that the census is based on the situation at the time of Solomon, not the earlier wilderness period.

were "273 firstborn Israelites who exceeded the number of Levites."[20] There were 22,000 Levites, so that means there were 22,273 firstborn Israelites at this time (Num 3:43). If there were only 22,273 firstborn, it would mean that there would have to be something like 50 to 100 individuals in a nuclear family for there to be a total population of 2 million.

There are further complications to consider when dealing with the numbers in Numbers (and elsewhere). These include the well-known fact that the Hebrew word *elef* ("thousand") which is used in Numbers has other possible meanings in this context, like "leader" or "troop." In short, it is overly dogmatic to insist that the Bible pictures two million people moving through the wilderness. Numbers in the biblical narrative frequently have purposes other than merely to communicate literal fact.

The other issue that is frequently discussed both in academic and, at least recently, in popular media has to do with the route of the wilderness wanderings. In terms of the book of Exodus, the main issue has to do with the location of Mount Sinai.

The Israelites left from the city of Rameses and set up camps successively at Succoth, Etham, and Pi-hahiroth between Migdol and the Sea, opposite Baal-zephon (Ex 12:37; 13:20-22; 14:1-9). After crossing the Sea, they came into the wilderness (Ex 15:22). The wilderness wanderings provide the geographical setting of the rest of the Pentateuch.

Their first major stopping area was Mount Sinai where Moses would receive the law as well as the instructions for the building of the tabernacle. They would stay in this location until Numbers 10:11. To reach Sinai, the Israelites camped at Marah, Elim, the wilderness of Sin, Dophkah, Alush and Rephidim (see Numbers 33 as well as citations in the book of Exodus). Unfortunately, we do not know the exact location of these sites, so we cannot reconstruct the exact route of their journey.

Three main theories include a northern route, a central route and a

---

[20]C. J. Humphreys, "The Number of People in the Exodus from Egypt: Decoding Mathematically the Very Large Numbers in Numbers 1 and 26," *Vetus Testamentum* 48 (1998): 196-213, and "The Numbers in the Exodus from Egypt: A Further Appraisal," *Vetus Testamentum* 50 (2000): 322-38.

southern route. The northern route, though, would have been discouraged by the presence of a strong Egyptian military presence. The middle route led right across Sinai's central limestone shield, but there were not adequate water supplies. The third route, the southern one, is the most likely route. If so, the traditional designation of Jebel Musa as Mount Sinai might be accurate. However, lately, amateur archaeologists have put forward the idea that Mount Sinai is to be located in what is today Saudi Arabia. While such an identification is not impossible, neither is it likely. In the final analysis, a precise and certain identification of Sinai is not possible, nor is it really important to our understanding of the event.

QUESTIONS FOR DISCUSSION

1. In this chapter, we have seen examples of deception to further the purposes of God (midwives; three-day journey). Can you think of any other examples from the Old Testament where there is deception that seems to further God's purposes?

2. How do you reconcile these stories of deception with the commandment not to bear false witness?

3. As we studied the plagues, we observed that the text itself acknowledged the existence of pagan gods (Ex 12:12). Was this surprising? How should we understand this in the light of other biblical teaching that the other gods are non-existent (Is 41:22-24; 42:9-20)?

4. Many modern liberation movements have used the exodus as a story of inspiration for their own efforts to throw off oppression. Some of these oppressed communities are religious but others are not. How legitimate is it for people today to cite the exodus in support of a modern political movement?

5. People today sometimes will say that they had a "burning bush" experience. What would they mean by this? Does God still speak to people in these dramatic and direct ways? Why or why not?

FOR FURTHER READING

See commentaries in appendix two.

Gowan, D. E. *Theology in Exodus: Biblical Theology in the Form of a Commentary.* Louisville: Westminster John Knox, 1994.

Langston, S. M. *Exodus Through the Centuries.* Oxford: Blackwell, 2006.

Williams, M. J. *Deception in Genesis: An Investigation into the Morality of a Unique Biblical Phenomenon.* New York: Peter Lang, 2001.

EIGHT

GOD GIVES ISRAEL HIS LAW

(Exodus 19–24)

Moses and the Israelites arrived at Mount Sinai (also called Horeb) two months after leaving Egypt (Ex 19:1). Of course, this area was the scene of Moses' commission at the burning bush (Ex 3:1). God had commanded Moses to bring his people here. Israel would stay here until they departed in Numbers 10:11.[1]

On his first trip up the mountain, Moses receives a message from God to give to the people. First he reminds them of the grace and status that he has granted them in the memorable words: "You know how I carried you on eagles' wings and brought you to myself" (Ex 19:4).[2] On this foundation of grace, he imparts his law to them: "Now if you obey me and keep my covenant" (Ex 19:5). And this is followed by the announcement of reward contingent on obedience: "you will be my own special treasure from among all the peoples on earth; for all the earth

---

[1]Peter Enns, *Exodus* (Grand Rapids: Zondervan, 2000) p. 186, points out that fifty-nine chapters are thus devoted to the time spent at Mount Sinai.

[2]For a penetrating analysis of this verse, see J. A. Davies, *A Royal Priesthood: Literary and Intertextual Perspectives on an Image of Israel in Exodus 19:6* (London: T & T Clark, 2004).

belongs to me. And you will be my kingdom of priests, my holy nation" (Ex 19:5-6). The pattern of grace, law and reward/punishment is a hallmark of the covenant and is repeated later in this section (and in places like Deuteronomy as well).

In terms of Exodus 19–24, however, these words are announcing the making of a new covenant between God and his people. It does not replace the previous Abrahamic covenant. This covenant, though, emphasizes human response in the form of law. We are, therefore, not surprised that at the time of its inauguration, the contents of these chapters are called the "Book of the Covenant" (Ex 24:7). Law is given in the context of covenant.[3]

THE TEN COMMANDMENTS

Whole books have been written on the Ten Commandments.[4] In this section, we will only be able to scratch the surface to bring out some of the leading ideas and set up our discussion of the case law as well as our later description of the relationship between the law and the New Testament.

The first thing to notice, and it is often missed, is the preamble to the Ten Commandments: "I am the LORD your God, who rescued you from the land of Egypt, the place of your slavery" (Ex 20:2). Though short and simple, God's statement is to the point. The following law flows from the foundation of an act of grace (a pattern noted above in Ex 19 as well). Israel's relationship with God is not initiated by observance of the law, but by God's sovereign act by which he freed them from bondage. In terms of the covenant/treaty structure—law follows the historical prologue where the sovereign, in this case God, retells the story of the relationship up to the present. Israel's obligation to keep the law is not to form a relationship with God, but rather to show gratitude to and maintain the relationship that it already enjoys with him.

---

[3]For covenant, see O. P. Robertson, *The Christ of the Covenants* (Phillipsburg, N.J.: P & R, 1981).

[4]The best in my opinion is by J. Douma, *The Ten Commandments: Manual for the Christian Life* (Phillipsburg, N.J.: P & R, 1996).

There are ten commandments. Later we will hear that God writes them on two stone tablets (Ex 31:18). Why two? Perhaps they could simply not be written on a single tablet. Traditionally, it has been imagined that one tablet held the commandments that dealt with the divine-human relationship (1 through 4) and the other held the commandments that regulate human-human relationships (5 through 10). However, based on analogy with ancient Near Eastern treaties (which forms the literary background of the covenant), it is thought that they might be two complete copies of all ten commandments. In ancient Near Eastern examples, the two copies of the treaty were placed in the temples of the two parties to the agreement, but here since there is only one God involved in this covenant/treaty between God and Israel both copies are placed in the Ark of the Covenant.[5]

Commandment 1. At the foundation of the law stands the demand that Yahweh, the God who brought Israel out of Egypt, will be their only God. Notice the formulation of this commandment does not insist that there is only one god. Indeed, we have seen in the first part of Exodus that the gods of Egypt were thought to exist and have some measure of power. Even so, Israel must not acknowledge them. They must worship only Yahweh.

Commandment 2. Israel is to be different from all the surrounding nations who worshiped their gods in the form of idols.[6] These idols were the object of worship, and though Mesopotamian theologians did not make a crass identification between their gods and the ornate statue that represented that god, the common people almost certainly did. These statues were clothed, bathed and fed. Israel's true God transcended such

---

[5]As argued in M. G. Kline, *Treaty of the Great King: The Covenant Structure of Deuteronomy* (Grand Rapids: Eerdmans, 1963).

[6]For interesting studies on idols in Mesopotamia, see W. W. Hallo, "Cult Statue and Divine Image: A Preliminary Study," in *Scripture in Context II: More Essays on the Comparative Method,* ed. W. W. Hallo, J. Moyer and L. Purdue (Winona Lake, Ind.: Eisenbrauns, 1983), pp. 1-18, and M. B. Dick, ed., *Born in Heaven Made on Earth: The Making of the Cult Image in the Ancient Near East* (Winona Lake, Ind.: Eisenbrauns, 1999). The most interesting study remains the chapter "The Care and Feeding of the Gods," in A. L. Oppenheim, *Ancient Mesopotamia: Portrait of a Dead Civilization* (Chicago: University of Chicago Press, 1977).

representation. Much later, Paul rightly described the heart of idolatry as the worship of the "things God created instead of the Creator himself" (Rom 1:25).

Interestingly, this commandment did not prohibit the use of highly potent symbols of God's presence. We will later see that the Ark of the Covenant is one such object. Apparently, the commandment does not forbid objects that represent God's presence, but the worship of these objects as if they were God himself.

Commandment 3. To "take God's name in vain" means to misuse that name. How one might misuse that name is not specified in the commandment, but would certainly include impulsive, angry cursing, flippancy or empty invocations of the name. It would certainly prohibit swearing to a falsehood in God's name. Conservative Jewish thinkers from ancient to modern times have often advocated never speaking the name of God. Today in some modern writing by conservative Jews, one sees an avoidance of the name Yahweh, which is replaced by such circumlocutions as "the Name," the Tetragrammaton (Four Letters), or G-d. One can doubt that the intention of the commandment was that the name would never be spoken. As we will observe from time to time, the application of the Commandments in the statutory law (see below) would suggest that the commandments had a positive side as well. While we should avoid misusing God's name, we should shout it out in loving praise.

Commandment 4. As we will see later, the Sabbath is something of an oddity in the Ten Commandments. It distinguishes the seventh day of the week as holy time in a similar way that the sanctuary of Israel is a holy place, the priests are holy people, and sacrifices are holy actions. In other words, the Sabbath is a part of the ceremonial law of the Old Testament, and as such it is unique in the Commandments. The interpretive issues surrounding the Sabbath are accordingly knotty and so is the question of its continuing application. For this reason, we will reserve a full discussion to chapter ten.

Commandment 5. The first of the commandments that regulate humans' relationships with other humans is one centered on the authority structure of the family. Children are to honor their parents. What honor means is not easy to specify, but will be spelled out in broad terms in the statutory law. It certainly means that one is to respect their parents and not hit or revile them (Ex 21:15, 17). It is interesting that the law uses the term "honor" and not the word "obey." This choice may be intentional since not all parents desire their children to obey God's law.

In the New Testament Paul points out that this is the first commandment that has a promise (Eph 6:2), and indeed in an important sense that is true. Continued existence in the Promised Land is contingent on honoring one's parents. However, Deuteronomy 27–28 makes it clear that the entire law is sanctioned by blessings and curses, so in another sense it is not the only law that has a promise (and a curse) attached to it.

Commandment 6. Often this commandment is wrongly thought to proscribe killing. Such a view would be impossible to reconcile with the rest of the Old Testament. God, after all, commands his people to kill in the context of judicial punishments and holy war. The commandment should thus be taken to forbid all killing which is not commanded by God. The first recorded murder is when Cain kills Abel, and God comes against the criminal with judgment. The covenant with Noah specifies that murderers must receive the ultimate punishment because the victim is created in the image of God, thus to kill another human is an assault against God himself. The case law exposits this commandment in a way that shows that it not only prohibits the taking of life, but it also promotes the creation of conditions that protect and enhance it as well.

Commandment 7. The prohibition of adultery is the foundation of sexual ethics in the Bible. Adultery is wrong because it infringes on the covenant of marriage and throws into question the paternity of a child who will inherit the family land.

Commandment 8. Private property is here protected by the command not to steal. Note that Israel had just lived through a period where they were totally under the control of the Egyptians. The Egyptians owned them, in essence not just stealing their possessions, but also their persons as they forced them to labor for no pay. The command not to steal also demonstrates that, no matter how egalitarian Israelite society was to be, especially in this early period, not all property was communally owned.

Commandment 9. Above (chapter 6), we pointed out instances where lies were honored with good results (i.e. the midwives lying to Pharaoh in Ex 1). The commandment is worded in a way that points to the court ("give false testimony"), but certainly it is not restricted to this venue as if it is all right to lie outside of a court. It is worded that way to reflect the profound consequences of lying in a court. Proverbs (Prov 6:16-19; 10:18; 12:17, 19, 22; 14:5, 25, etc.) makes it clear that society must be built on the truth and not falsehood. However, as already suggested in the previous chapter, the truth in certain contexts can produce tremendous damage and lead to incredible evil. Some people may relinquish the right to the truth due to the purpose for which they intend to use it. In such instances they are no longer a "neighbor."

Commandment 10. Up to this point, the Ten Commandments require external behavior. However with the commandment not to covet the entire law is internalized. Obedience requires more than simply restraint from murder, adultery and stealing. Hate that wants to take a life, lust that wants to have intercourse with another woman, desire to have something that belongs to another person—all of these are prohibited by the commandment not to covet.

THE CASE LAW

While everyone has heard (though they may not be able to name) the Ten Commandments, the case law is foreign to a modern Christian audience. If a modern reader knows the law "You must not cook a young goat in its mother's milk" (Ex 23:19), they would likely be hard pressed to know what to make of it. While not every law is as opaque in its meaning as this one, the modern relevance of these laws is a persistent question.

In Exodus, the case laws follow hard on the heels of the Ten Commandments and are found in 20:22–23:19. They cover a range of topics: proper worship ritual, slavery, marriage, theft, violence, dangerous animals, relationship with parents and more.

While the Ten Commandments are phrased as universally valid ethical principles to the covenant community, the case law cites specific
instances of offense. Indeed, upon closer examination, one can detect a
connection between the Ten Commandments and the various case laws.
*The case laws are applications of the principles of the Ten Commandments
to the specific social and redemptive historical situation of Israel.*

Sometimes the connection is obvious, as for example the altar law:

> *Build for me an altar made of earth, and offer your sacrifices to me—your
> burnt offerings and peace offerings, your sheep and goats, and your cattle.
> Build my altar wherever I cause my name to be remembered, and I will come
> to you and bless you. If you use stones to build my altar, use only natural,
> uncut stones. Do not shape the stones with a tool, for that would make the
> altar unfit for holy use. And do not approach my altar by going up steps. If you
> do, someone might look up under your clothing and see your nakedness.* (Ex
> 20:24-26)

This law shows God's concern for how he is worshiped. It is an application of the second commandment that forbids the construction of idols. An
altar could easily become an idol, especially if it was engraved or shaped
with a tool. We can also detect what we might call an anti-Canaanite po-
lemic (a theme that plays an important role in the law). When it forbids
steps to prevent a glance at the private parts of a priest, it is avoiding even
a hint of the sexual practices associated with Baal worship.

A second example would be the goring-ox law of Exodus 21:28-36, a
passage too long to cite so we will summarize the main points. The law
demands the death of an ox that gores someone to death. If the ox is allowed to live and kills a second person, then not only must the ox be
killed, but also the owner (though there is the possibility of a lesser
punishment, more about this later). The principle applied here is the
sixth commandment. What does "You must not murder" mean when an
ox gores someone to death?

However, sometimes the connection between a case law and a commandment (or multiple commandments) is not so clear, such as in the
case of boiling a young goat in its mother's milk (see above). What are
we to make of this law? While we cannot be dogmatic in detail, the law

is likely connected to Israel's ritual since it appears at the end of a section of the case law describing the proper worship associated with the three annual festivals of Israel (Ex 23:14-19a). At one point, the conundrum was thought definitively solved in the light of an Ugaritic text that seemed to mention this practice. Even though that text has been understood in a different way, it seems best to speculate that this law, like the altar law, does distance Israelite practice from Canaanite practice and thus would be a specific application of the first two commandments.

These examples intend to demonstrate that the case laws are applications of the principles of the Ten Commandments to specific situations in the life of ancient Israel. Recognizing this will aid us as we try to understand whether and in what way these laws speak to us today (see chapter 10). But before we approach this question, we should get a bit fuller understanding of the case law.

A law for the wilderness. According to Exodus, the law came to Moses in the wilderness. However, some of the laws would not be relevant for wilderness life. They presume life in the land.

Is it likely, for instance, that the wilderness generation kept slaves (Ex 21:2-11)? For that matter, how many bulls were likely found in the wilderness camp (Ex 21:28-36)? Certainly there were no vineyards or fields in which livestock could graze (Ex 22:5). No one owned fields so that if they were burned down by another there would be an issue of restitution (Ex 22:6). Other examples could be given.

Some people read these laws and argue that they could not have originated during the wilderness period. They had to be written later when they were in the land. They use this insight to argue against a wilderness origin for the Book of the Covenant and thus against Mosaic authorship of any of the law.

In response, we must first acknowledge that the premise of the argument is correct. Some of the laws presuppose a settled existence. However, there is more than one way to question the conclusion that the entire law must therefore be a product of a period later than the Mosaic.

In the first place, the law could be supplemented. In appendix one, we recognize clear postmosaic additions to the Pentateuch. While it is important to insist on a Mosaic foundation of the law as well as the Pentateuch, that does not rule out the possibility that the law was updated by supplements.

However, we may not even need to have recourse to the possibility of updating. Why shouldn't the law anticipate settled life? When the Israelites received the law, they were heading toward the Promised Land. Even though they were delayed from entry into the land due to their rebellion, they were always expecting to go into the land and begin a settled existence with fields, vineyards, slaves and the other accoutrements of life in the land. Thus, the argument that the law implies a settled existence is not a strong argument against its origins in the wilderness.

The penalties of the law. Penalties sanction the laws of the book of the covenant.[7] Most of the laws specify punishment that follows their transgression. The two most common penalties named in the law are restitution and capital punishment.

In matters of theft, the law requires the criminal to pay back the loss with interest. The theft of an ox or sheep requires the payment of five ox or sheep if the animal is slaughtered or sold, two if it is still alive in the thief's possession (Ex 22:1, 4). In this way, the criminals do not profit (provided they are caught), and the victims are compensated for their loss. If criminals do not have the wherewithal to pay back the victim, then they are sold into slavery to pay for their crime (Ex 22:3). If the criminal was uncooperative, they were likely put to death (Deut 21:18-21).

Many crimes were punishable by death: murder (Ex 21:14), assault on one's parents or cursing them (Ex 21:15, 16), being the owner of an ox that gores a person to death for a second time (Ex 21:29), and the list goes on and on.

Even though the penalty is stated in what appears to be absolute terms ("must be put to death"), internal evidence exists that suggests that lesser punishments could be applied in these "capital cases." A clear example of such flexibility is in the law of the goring ox (Ex 21:28-32). According to

---

[7]For a full discussion of the penalties of the law and their relevance for today, see my "God's Law and Mosaic Punishments Today," in *Theonomy: A Reformed Critique*, ed. W. S. Barker and W. R. Godfrey (Grand Rapids: Zondervan, 1990), pp. 41-57.

this law, if an ox gores and kills a second time after a warning, the owner is to be put to death. However, there is the possibility that he can pay a ransom. It is vague as to who can allow a lesser punishment, but it is likely that it is the judge in consultation with the victim's kin.

The awareness of the possibility of a lesser penalty in connection with the goring ox law leads to another interesting passage.[8] "Also, you must never accept a ransom payment for the life of someone judged guilty of murder and subject to execution; murderers must always be put to death. And never accept a ransom payment from someone who has fled to a city of refuge, allowing a slayer to return to his property before the death of the high priest" (Num 35:31-32).

It appears from these passages that ransoms were a possibility for many other crimes. Only murder required the application of the death penalty according to Pentateuchal law.

QUESTIONS FOR DISCUSSION

1. Read through the entire case law in Exodus 20:22–23:19. For each law ask "To which commandment(s) is this case law related?"

2. Anticipating our discussion of the modern Christian use of the law in chapter eleven, ask yourself how these laws and their penalties might apply today if at all.

3. Do these laws seem fair to you? Why or why not?

4. What do these laws say about God?

5. What do the punishments say about God's attitude toward these sins/crimes?

FOR FURTHER READING

Barker, W. S., and W. R. Godfrey, eds. *Theonomy: A Reformed Critique.* Grand Rapids: Zondervan, 1990.

---

[8]See J. Jordan, "The Death Penalty in the Mosaic Law: Five Exploratory Essays" (Biblical Horizons Occasional Paper No. 3, 1988), p. 10.

Douma, J. *The Ten Commandments: Manual for the Christian Life*. Phillipsburg, N.J.: P & R, 1996.

Kaiser, Walter. *Toward Old Testament Ethics*. Grand Rapids: Zondervan, 1983.

Patrick, D. *Old Testament Law*. Atlanta: Westminster John Knox, 1985.

Wright, Christopher J. H. *Old Testament Ethics for the People of God*. Downers Grove, Ill.: InterVarsity Press, 2004.

NINE

GOD INSTRUCTS ISRAEL
TO BUILD THE TABERNACLE

(Exodus 25–40)

oses received more than the law while on Mount Sinai. God also
gave him the plans for a structure in which he would make his presence
known to his people. Yahweh was not a god like those of the surrounding nations. The nations constructed images of their gods (see above)
and thought that their gods were actually resident in those objects. The
law prohibited the construction of such images (Ex 20:4-6); nonetheless, Yahweh directed the construction of a sanctuary to which the people could come and experience his palpable presence. This structure is
known as the tabernacle.

DIVINE INITIATIVE

The book of Exodus carefully guards the idea that it is Yahweh himself
who initiates the construction of the tabernacle. It would be inappropri-
ate for human beings to initiate the building of a holy place. David found
this out at a later point of history, when God reprimanded him for initi-
ating the building of the temple (2 Sam 7:5-7).

Not only did God initiate the idea of the tabernacle while Moses was on Mount Sinai, he also provided the plans. In the divine instructions to build the tabernacle, God repeatedly reminded Moses to build the tabernacle and its furnishings exactly according to the pattern God had shown him (Ex 25:8, 40; 26:30; 27:8).

In addition, God provided the materials with which to construct the building. After all, one wonders where a people wandering in the wilderness after many years in slavery happened to get the precious metals, woods and materials needed to construct such an ornate building. The answer comes in the so-called "plundering of the Egyptians" episode. As they were leaving Egypt, they "stripped the Egyptians of their wealth" (Ex 12:35-36).

And God provided more than the precious materials. He even gave the skilled craftsmen their abilities. Bezalel, son of Uri, and Oholiab, son of Ahisamach, were the two chief craftsmen in charge. God gave them "the Spirit of God" which gave them "great wisdom, ability and expertise in all kinds of crafts" (Ex 31:3).

From start to finish, the tabernacle was a God-given structure. The people of God were charged to follow the instructions that God gave them with the materials and skill he provided. The structure of the narrative demonstrates how they followed these instructions to a tee. In Exodus 25–31, God presents the instructions in the imperative, and Exodus 35–40 report the detailed observance of God's command. Even so, between the command and its fulfillment Israel lost its way and almost did not recover.

THREAT TO PROPER WORSHIP: THE GOLDEN CALF (EXODUS 32–34)

While Moses was on the Mount receiving instructions for proper worship of the true God, the Israelites under Aaron's leadership perversely worshiped a golden calf. The people quickly lost confidence in God after Moses was absent from the camp, up on the mountain. They urged Aaron to construct a calf image.

Ambiguity surrounds the significance of the image. When the idol was formed from the people's golden earrings, Aaron announced, "O Israel, these are the *elohim* who brought you out of the land of Egypt!" (Ex 32:4). Most English translations render *elohim* in the plural "gods," thus indicating that the calf represents a false deity. If true, the identity of the deity is obscure. One might think of Baal, who often is described as a bull in Ugaritic literature. But according to this translation, Aaron speaks of "gods" in the plural. However, why would one calf image represent plural gods?

For this reason, some scholars suggest that a better translation would be "this is the god who brought you out of the land of Egypt" and argue that this God is none other than Yahweh. After all, *elohim* is often translated in the singular in reference to Yahweh. If this interpretation is correct, then the calf either represents Yahweh or even was considered the pedestal on which the invisible presence of Yahweh stood.

On one level, a decision on these matters is unimportant. To worship Yahweh in such an unauthorized way would be a heinous sin, equal to worshiping a false god. Israel was engaged in the false worship of an idol whether the image was of Baal, Yahweh or some other deity.

Thus, when Moses descended from the mountain and saw them perversely worshiping an image, he angrily threw the two tablets of the law to the ground, shattering them. Israel had broken the covenant through their actions and Moses' shattering the tablets represented the breaking of relationship between God and Israel.

Indeed, God intended to eradicate the rebellious Israelites and start all over again; Moses would become the new Abraham (Ex 32:9-10). However, Moses, the prophet, interceded with Yahweh, invoking the promises given to Abraham, and thus turned away God's destructive wrath.

Israel would thus continue to be God's people, but not without consequences. Moses called for volunteers to enact God's justice against those who broke fellowship with God. The Levites responded and executed about 3,000 of their fellow Israelites who worshiped the Golden Calf. For their work, Moses ordained the Levites for priestly service to the Lord (see below on the staff of the tabernacle).

Thus, relationship is restored between Israel and its forgiving God.

Yahweh shows that he will continue to be present to Moses by giving him a revelation of his glory (Ex 33:12-23) and God presents Moses with new copies of the covenant treaty in the form of two stone tablets.

THE SHAPE OF PROPER WORSHIP
(EXODUS 25–31; 35–40)

Though interrupted by the potentially disastrous Golden Calf episode, the bulk of the last part of Exodus is devoted to the instructions and then the description of the construction of the tabernacle. The symbolic significance of the tabernacle derives from its form.

A tent. Though ornate, the tabernacle is a tent. It has wooden sides over which hang four coverings that are held down by tent pegs.

The form of God's house thus conforms to that of the people. The people live in a tent and so God lives in a tent. As we will see, this conforms to a principle that runs through Scripture that *the shape of God's place of worship conforms to the social and redemptive-historical status of the people of God.* The temple, a permanent structure, replaces the tabernacle, a mobile one, only when the Israelites have peace from all their internal enemies (see chapter 12).

The shape of the tabernacle structure. The tabernacle was initially constructed as the tribes moved through the wilderness area. Numbers 2 describes the layout of the camp and informs us that the tabernacle was placed in the middle of the camp with three tribes on each side and the Levites camped immediately around the tabernacle area. The center of the camp was an appropriate place for the structure that represents God's dwelling since in the ancient Near East the king or war leader's tent would occupy the central location, surrounded by his bodyguard (the Levites) and then the rest of the army.

A finely woven curtain set on posts with bronze bases separated the tabernacle area from the rest of the camp (Ex 27:1-19). The curtain created a courtyard that was 150 feet long and 75 feet wide. The eastern and western ends were the short ones. The tabernacle faced east so an entrance indicated by an ornate curtain, resembling the innermost curtain of the tabernacle itself (see pp. 136-37), faced east. The eastern orientation is never explained but does put the tabernacle in the direction of the rising sun.

The tabernacle was not a large building. From the size and number of the frames that formed the north and south side, it appears to be about thirty feet long, and from those that composed its west side, it was approximately ten feet wide. Its height was fifteen feet (see Ex 26:15-25). It had two parts, the last third being the Holy of Holies. When we discuss the furniture of the tabernacle, we will see that the Ark of the Covenant, the most potent symbol of God's presence, was kept there. The Ark is the footstool of God's throne, thus signifying that the room itself was the divine throne room. As its name indicates, the Holy of Holies was the place of most intense holiness in the camp.

Gradations of holiness. As the place where God chose to make his presence known, the tabernacle was holy ground. The primary meaning of holiness in Hebrew (*qdsh* and its derivatives) is "to be set apart." Sin created a barrier that separated humans from God. Humans could not casually approach God without dire consequences, but they had to be mindful of their sin and offer a sacrifice under the guidance of a priest.

The very structure and symbolic significance of the tabernacle proclaimed the presence of a holy God in the midst of a sinful camp. God dwelt in the Holy of Holies and thus zones of holiness emanated from that place outward. As one moved toward the center, one entered places of increased holiness. William Propp has used the helpful analogy of a nuclear reactor to illustrate this point. As one moves closer and closer to the core, one gets bombarded by increasing levels of radiation.[1] In a similar manner, as one moves closer and closer to the Holy of Holies, one encounters increasing levels of holiness.

The metals. This increasing holiness is communicated through the metals that are used for the construction of the tabernacle. Moving from the outside in, we see a change from the use of bronze to silver to gold to pure gold. The posts that hold up the courtyard curtain have bronze bases and the curtains are hung with silver hooks and rings (Ex 27:10-

---

[1]Propp, personal communication.

11). Moving closer to the center, the frames that constitute the sidewalls of the tabernacle are silver (Ex 26:19-21). Inside the tabernacle, we find gold and in the Holy of Holies everything is made from the purest gold. The increased preciousness of the metals reflects the increasing levels of holiness, indicating the presence of God in the Holy of Holies.

Levels of access. Increasingly holiness also means further restrictions on access. Gentiles and unclean Israelites live outside the camp.[2] Israel lives inside the camp, but only the Levites encamp in the immediate vicinity of the tabernacle and they also have the easiest access to its holy precincts. But even the priests have restrictions. Indeed, according to Leviticus 16, only one man, the high priest, only once a year could enter the Holy of Holies, indicating just how holy (set apart) it was.[3]

The curtains of the tabernacle: heaven on earth. Exodus 26:1-14 describes the four curtains of the tabernacle. The three outermost curtains have no symbolic function, but serve to protect the elaborate innermost curtain from the weather. The outermost curtain is of debated material, the Hebrew word being rare. The NLT translates "fine goatskin leather," while other suggestions include the hide of the sea cow, the porpoise, the dolphin, the dugong. All of these would serve the purpose of weatherproofing well, as do the next two curtains, "tanned ram skins" and "goat-hair cloth."

Most attention is focused on the innermost curtain. This is the curtain that would be seen from the interior of the tabernacle. The material is described as "blue, purple, and scarlet thread and with skillfully embroidered cherubim" (Ex 26:1). The cherubim are heavenly beings that often are found close to God and are likely to be understood as God's bodyguards. They protect access to the Holy God.

In any case, as we imagine ourselves standing in the tabernacle and looking up in the light of the menorah, we can understand the signifi-

---

[2]Not all uncleanness required removal from the camp, but some did (Num 5:1-4).
[3]Of course, this raises the question as to how the tent could be taken down once erected. If no one could enter the Holy of Holies except the High Priest on the Day of Atonement, then how could objects like the Ark of the Covenant be removed for the march? It may be that there were ceremonies unmentioned in Scripture that, when performed, rendered the area accessible to the Levites responsible for moving the tent (Num 4).

cance of the blue roof with the flying cherubim. We are in heaven; the tabernacle is heaven on earth. The author of the book of Hebrews understood this when he stated concerning the High Priests of the Old Testament, "They serve in a system of worship that is only a copy, a shadow of the real one in heaven."

The furniture. God is the king of the world. He dwells in heaven,[4] but he makes his presence known in the world by commanding Israel to construct his home on earth. As king, his home is a palace, but it is a home nonetheless. As a home, it has furniture. The furniture itself has tremendous symbolic significance.

The Ark of the Covenant. The Ark was a box that was 45 inches long, 27 inches wide, and 27 inches high (Ex 25:10-22, see v. 10). While relatively small, it was constructed of the finest acacia wood and overlain with pure gold. It had gold rings on its side through which poles could be inserted in order to carry the box without actually touching it.

While the Ark did not have imposing dimensions, it was an object of incredible symbolic power. It was placed in the most central place in the Holy of Holies and later Scripture refers to it as God's footstool (1 Chron 28:2) and even his throne (Jer 3:16-17). For this reason, Exodus describes the construction of two cherubim statues whose outstretched wings touched over the Ark. Their heads face down because the glory of God was above them (25:18-20).

The Ark was also a container. Exodus 25:21 mentions that the stone tablets with "the terms of the covenant" were placed inside of it. Thus, the Ark contained the document that provided the foundation of the relationship between God and his people.

The menorah. Inside God's house was a source of light, the menorah (Ex 25:31-40). The tent would have been very dark without it. It is described as having a center stem as well as six branches going out from the center stem, seven lights in all.

In terms of its symbolic value, we need to direct attention to the floral imagery associated with it. "Craft the center stem of the lampstand with

---

[4]Though "even the highest heavens cannot contain you" (1 Kings 8:27).

four lamp cups shaped like almond blossoms, complete with buds and petals" (Ex 25:34). The menorah is essentially a tree.

That the place of God's presence is associated with a tree should not be surprising. After all, the place where humans and God fellowshipped freely with each other was in a garden, the Garden of Eden. The tabernacle, thus, represents the Garden of Eden as well as heaven on earth.

The incense altar. The constant offering of sacrifices with the manipulation of the blood of the animals would have resulted in a putrid odor were it not for the incense altar (Ex 30:1-10). Like the Ark of the Covenant, the incense altar was small but precious. Measuring 18 inches square and 36 inches high, it was covered with pure gold. It was placed just outside the inner curtain that separated the Holy of Holies from the rest of the sanctuary. A special formula was used for the incense that was burned on this altar (Ex 30:34-38), prohibited from outside use.

The table of the bread of the presence. A small table (36 inches wide, 18 inches deep, 27 inches high) was also placed in the tabernacle (Ex 25:23-30). It was made of precious acacia wood and covered with pure gold. The "bread of the presence" was placed on it. From the description in Exodus, we recognize that it functioned as a table for dining, though of course there is no idea of God eating the bread. The bread of the presence is not described in Exodus, but it is in Leviticus 24:5-9. Here we see that each week the priests are to eat the old bread and replace it with twelve fresh loaves. The fact that there are twelve loaves surely represents the twelve tribes of Israel, and that it is called the bread of the presence indicates that the twelve tribes are in the presence of God. Further, we might speculate that there is a connection with the covenant. After all, agreements like a covenant relationship were ratified or celebrated by eating a meal together. The loaves were thus a reminder of the intimate relationship that Israel enjoyed with their covenant Lord.

The sacrificial altar. Outside the tabernacle proper stood the bronze altar of sacrifice (Ex 27:1-8). It was here that the Israelites offered sacrifices such as those described in Leviticus 1-7. The altar was seven-and-a-half feet wide and long and four-and-a-half feet high. The corners had "horns," referring to rounded protrusions on the side of the altar. The function of the horns is not clear, though some believe they were used to tie down the sacrificial animal. However, such an action seems unnecessary because the animals were killed before being put on the altar.

The altar was analogous to a cooking stove in a regular home. Again, though, there is no idea that God actually ate the sacrifices, though some of the sacrifices were consumed by the priests and even the worshipers who offered them.

The washbasin. Also like a regular house, the tabernacle had a washbasin. It was placed between the sacrificial altar and the tabernacle. The priests were required to wash their hands as they moved from the altar to the tabernacle. Coming into the presence of the Lord required great respect and cleanliness.

The staff: the priests. The tabernacle is thus the house of God on earth. He is the heavenly king and the tabernacle is the king's dwelling. Of course, the king has attendants at his house, those servants who care and maintain it on behalf of their royal master. The book of Exodus tells us that the Levites assume that position. They get the job because of their actions at the time of the Golden Calf fiasco. Interestingly, there is a backstory to the events of Exodus 32–34 that takes us to Genesis 34, the story of the rape of Dinah.

Dinah's two full brothers were Simeon and Levi, so when she was raped by the local Canaanite ruler, Prince Shechem, it was a matter of grave concern to them. Shechem, as it turns out, wanted to marry her, and so he came and presented his case to the family. Simeon and Levi insisted that if they were to be married that not only Shechem but all the men of the city needed to be circumcised to fit in with the customs of their family. Perhaps indicating his honest feelings toward Dinah, the prince agreed to this painful procedure for himself and his people.

Simeon and Levi, however, had a darker purpose in mind. Once the people of Shechem were weakened by the removal of their foreskins, the two sons of Jacob went through the city massacring the men. Jacob was unaware of their plans, however, and was furious at them. They have made the family odious to the local Canaanites and thus they would have to move.

The reticent narrator never adjudicates between Jacob and his sons. Even so, he may have shown his hand when he allows the sons the last word, "Should he have treated our sister like a prostitute!" (Gen 34:33).

Nonetheless, at the end of his life, Jacob had the opportunity to curse his two violence-prone sons in his "last will and testament":

> *Simeon and Levi are two of a kind,*
> > *their weapons are instruments of violence.*
> *May I never join them in their meetings;*
> > *may I never be a party to their plans.*
> *For in their anger they murdered men,*
> > *and they crippled oxen just for sport.*
> *A curse on their anger for it is fierce,*
> > *a curse on their wrath for it is cruel.*
> *I will scatter them among the descendants of Jacob.*
> > *I will disperse them throughout Israel. (Gen 49:5-7)*

For their violence, they will be spread throughout the land and not given a territorial allotment. The devastating consequence of such a move is that they would lose their identity as a distinct tribe within Israel.

If we fast forward to the book of Joshua, we see that neither Levi nor Simeon is given a distinct tribal territory, but cities within the boundaries of other tribes (Josh 13:14; 19:1-9; 21). Indeed, Simeon was ultimately absorbed within the tribe of Judah. Levi, on the other hand, became the most distinctive tribe in spite of their scattering, and this, of course, because of the priestly function conferred on them by Moses in Exodus 32.

What is often missed though is the connection between these stories and how these texts help illuminate the priestly function. In a word, the Golden Calf episode demonstrates how the Levites could channel their violent tendencies in a God-honoring way. In response to Moses' call, they went out and killed 3,000 of their fellow Israelites, thus showing they were the perfect candidates for the priesthood. After all, the priests are the guardians or bodyguards of God's holiness. They protected the sanctity of the tabernacle, serving as gatekeepers and facilitating rituals like sacrifice which appeased God's anger toward the sin of his people. They taught the law so that people would not ignorantly offend God, and the High Priest manipulated the Urim and Thummim (Ex 28:30).

The finale: the glory cloud. The book of Exodus concludes with the notification that the tabernacle was constructed exactly as God had ordered Moses to do it (Ex 40:1-33). Once all was set in place, God moved in as was symbolized by the cloud covering that hovered over it as the glory of God filled the tabernacle (Ex 40:34-38). The cloud had been with them since they left Egypt, but now it settled in the tabernacle, departing only to lead them on their journey. The cloud that burned at night became known as the Shekinah (from the Hebrew verb *shkn* "to dwell") Glory cloud in Jewish tradition. It represented God's presence.

As we saw in chapter three, the presence of God is one of the most, if not the most, important theme in the book of Exodus. While at the beginning of the book, God was not explicitly present with the people, by the end of the book, God had established an abiding symbol of his presence in the camp. In essence, the book of Exodus has been driving to this point, and thus the narrative concludes with a strong sense of closure. The people are freed from bondage. They have entered into a covenant with God that establishes them as a nation. Now the tabernacle is fully constructed and God has made his presence known by covering the tabernacle with the cloud.

However, like Genesis before it, the ending of this second chapter of the Pentateuch also anticipates the future by anticipating the journey that will be narrated in Leviticus, Numbers and Deuteronomy:

> *Now whenever the cloud lifted from the Tabernacle, the people of Israel would set out on their journey, following it. But if the cloud did not rise, they remained where they were until it lifted. The cloud of the LORD hovered over the Tabernacle during the day, and at night fire glowed inside the cloud so the whole family of Israel could see it. This continued throughout all their journeys. (Ex 40:36-38)*

QUESTIONS FOR DISCUSSION

1. Summarize the ways in which the tabernacle demonstrated God's presence to the people of Israel.

2. The chapter described God's tent as analogous to a human tent with stove, table and footstool. Reflect on why God would make his presence known in such a way.

3. Some authors take a more allegorical approach to the symbolism of the tabernacle. For instance, the blue colors of the tabernacle curtain point to Christ's royalty, the large entrance refers to Christ's inviting outstretched arms.[5] Do you see any weaknesses in such an approach?

FOR FURTHER READING

Haran, M. *Temples and Temple Service in Ancient Israel: An Investigation into Biblical Cult Phenomena and the Historical Setting of the Priestly School.* Winona Lake, Ind.: Eisenbrauns, 1985.

Longman, Tremper, III. *Immanuel in Our Place: Seeing Christ in Israel's Worship.* Phillipsburg, N.J.: P & R, 2001.

---

[5]See, for instance, P. F. Kiene, *The Tabernacle of God in the Wilderness of Sinai* (Grand Rapids: Zondervan, 1977).

5

READING EXODUS

AS A CHRISTIAN

■   ■   ■

The next part of our study of Exodus should not be taken to mean that Christians do not or should not read the book as we have been reading it in the past nine chapters. As Brevard Childs stated it, it is vitally important for the Christian to honor the "discrete witness" of the Old Testament.[1] We should read it first as if we lived in the period of time before Jesus Christ. As we have seen above, we do this best when we take account of its ancient Near Eastern setting, including reading the book in the light of the literary conventions of the day.

---

[1]B. S. Childs, *Biblical Theology of the Old and New Testaments: Theological Reflection on the Christian Bible* (Minneapolis: Fortress, 1992), pp. 95-118.

Childs, for one, would not have the Christian stop after doing this initial reading. The Christian affirms the fact that God climactically spoke to his people through his son Jesus Christ and that the New Testament is witness to this revelation. The New Testament does not replace the Old Testament, but rather fulfills it. In the famous words of Saint Augustine, "The New Testament is in the Old concealed. The Old Testament is in the New revealed."

Of course, much more significant for the Christian are the words of Jesus himself. It is of note that during the brief period of Jesus' post-resurrection appearances to his disciples, he chose twice to address the question of the Old Testament witness to his death and resurrection. The gist of this teaching is that "everything written about me in the law of Moses and the prophets and in the Psalms must be fulfilled" (Lk 24:44). He even demonstrated this reading of the Old Testament to them: "Then Jesus took them through the writings of Moses and all the prophets, explaining from all the Scriptures the things concerning himself" (Lk 24:27).

As part of the "writings of Moses," the Christian should be attentive to how the book of Exodus anticipates the coming of Jesus Christ. As we do so, we marvel at how the New Testament guides us to a proper appreciation of how Jesus fulfills the exodus (chapter 10), the law (chapter 11), and the tabernacle (chapter 12).

TEN

THE CHRISTIAN EXPERIENCE
OF EXODUS

The exodus was the most important salvation event of the Old Testament. God rescued his people from Egyptian bondage by miraculous and extraordinary means. The crossing of the Sea is the climactic moment of their rescue. They had no human means to escape Egypt, but God himself provided the way out. We should not be surprised that the significance of such an important event reverberates through the rest of the Old Testament and into the New Testament.

While the Christian experience of the exodus is explained by reference to the New Testament, later Old Testament texts anticipate and prepare for the use of the tradition in the New. We will begin by looking at the re-actualizations of the Sea crossing at the Jordan River and at the time of Elijah's death, then we will acknowledge the use of the exodus in the Psalms. Next, we will explore the theme of the exodus in the prophets of the eighth and sixth centuries B.C. Finally, we will map out its culminating use in the New Testament.

FORTY YEARS LATER (JOSHUA 3)
After the crossing of the Sea, Israel continued its trek toward Canaan

through the wilderness. At Kadesh-Barnea, Moses sent twelve tribes into the land. They reported that the land was lush and fertile, but also occupied by fearsome warriors. The people's lack of confidence in God at that moment doomed them to forty years of wandering. The time period was such that the first generation died there and did not enter the land. Thus, after forty years, as the second generation stood on the bank of the Jordan ready to cross, they had not personally experienced the dramatic and powerful intervention of God at the Sea.

Thus, as the people under the leadership of Joshua crossed the Jordan for the first time to enter the Promised Land, the Jordan River stopped flowing so they could walk across on dry land. The waters stopped flowing and they began to pile up the second that the priests who were carrying the Ark stepped in. God was using this event to demonstrate to his people that he, the God of power and rescue, was still with them as they began the fight against their formidable enemy, the Canaanites.

ELIJAH'S ASCENT (2 KINGS 2)

In the ninth century B.C., beginning with the reign of Ahab and his queen Jezebel, Israel had a fascination with the worship of Baal. Baal was a god of the previous inhabitants of the land (Canaanites, Phoenicians and others) who controlled the waters. He defeated the Sea, and he distributed the waters as the god of rain and dew. In response to this threat to his sole worship, God raised up Elijah to confront the forces of Baal. When Elijah's work was over, God sent a chariot to bring him to heaven. God also raised up a successor named Elisha who would continue the fight against paganism.

Many of the actions and miracles associated with Elijah and Elisha have to do with water. In this way, God showed that it was not Baal but himself who controlled the waters. Just before Elijah ascended to heaven, Elisha followed him wherever he went. Among the amazing things that he witnessed was the dividing of the Jordan River when Elijah struck it with his garment. After his death, Elisha's succession is symbolized by his inheriting this garment with which he too struck the Jordan River. The fact that it again divided to allow him to walk on dry ground testified to his status as Elijah's successor. The God of power who was with Elijah was the same God of power who was at the Sea. He was now the God of power who supported Elisha.

REMEMBRANCE OF THE EXODUS IN THE PSALMS

In chapter five, we examined Psalm 77 to demonstrate that the later appropriation of the exodus tradition depends on its historicity. In the process, of course, the psalmist here demonstrates the remembrance of the event in prayer. The exodus in that psalm gave the psalmist confidence in the midst of present troubles and hope for the future because God delivered his people at the Sea in the past.

Psalm 114 invokes the memory of the exodus, but for a different purpose:

> *When the Israelites escaped from Egypt—*
> *   when the family of Jacob left that foreign land—*
> *the land of Judah became God's sanctuary,*
> *   and Israel became his kingdom.*
>
> *The Red Sea saw them coming and hurried out of their way!*
> *   The water of the Jordan River turned away.*
> *The mountains skipped like rams,*
> *   the hills like lambs!*
> *What's wrong, Red Sea, that made you hurry out of their way?*
> *   What happened, Jordan River, that you turned away?*
>
> *Why mountains, did you skip like rams?*
> *   Why, hills, like lambs?*
> *Tremble, O earth, at the presence of the LORD,*
> *   at the presence of the God of Jacob.*
> *He turned the rock into a pool of water;*
> *   yes, a spring of water flowed from solid rock.*

The tone of the psalm is celebratory and challenging. The psalmist celebrates God's choice of Israel and its rescue from Egypt and establishment in the land. Interestingly, the waters of the Re(e)d Sea and the Jordan River are personified (as we saw in Psalm 77). This combines the historical tradition of the exodus with the mythological motif of God's battle and subjugation of the waters of chaos to create a quite vivid and exciting and powerful picture of God and his rescue of Israel. The psalm challenges others by reminding the rest of the earth of this powerful God's interest in his people. Of course, only Israelites would have heard this psalm, so the actual effect on the audience would be one of comfort and assurance in the midst of threat.

THE SECOND EXODUS

The exodus was an event that occurred at the beginning of Israel's history. Later Israelites looked back on the event to garner courage to live in their own turbulent present. However, the eighth and sixth century prophets appropriate the language of the exodus in a new and unexpected way. They speak of the exodus as if it were a future event!

Hosea, an eighth-century prophet, majored on oracles of judgment. Israel had committed spiritual adultery against their God and now they would suffer the consequences. However, judgment would not be the end of Israel's story. God looks back on the wonderful relationship that he enjoyed with his people upon their release from captivity in Egypt. Judgment is imagined as a sort of reversion to wilderness times. And just as at the time of the historical exodus and wilderness, so he will once again bring his people into the Promised Land. Only this time their entry will be smooth. The Valley of Achor (Trouble), so named because of Achan's sin after the battle at Jericho (Josh 7), will be a gateway of hope (Hos 2:14-16).

No prophetic book utilizes the second exodus theme more pervasively than Isaiah (see Is 4:5; 11:15-16; 40:1-11; 43:18-19; 48:21; 49:11-12; 50:2; 51:9-10; 52:10; 63:11-14). For our purposes, the most important of these occurrences is in 40:1-11, in which context we read:

> Listen! It's the voice of someone shouting,
>   "Clear the way through the wilderness for the LORD!
> Make a straight highway through the wasteland
>   for our God!
> Fill the valleys,

> *and level the mountains and hills.*
> *Straighten the curves,*
>   *and smooth out the rough places.*
> *Then the glory of the* Lord *will be revealed,*
>   *and all the people will see it together.*
>   *The* Lord *has spoken!" (Is 40:3-5)*

After being cast out from the land, they now return. God will make this second entry from the wilderness easier than the first. The wilderness was a rough area and very difficult to travel due to high mountains and deep ravines. God will cause the former to flatten and the latter to fill up, so in essence the people of God will enjoy a superhighway to end their second exodus.

The sixth-century prophets may not develop the theme as extensively as Isaiah but echoes of the exodus may certainly be seen in a prophet like Jeremiah. In Jeremiah 16:14-15 and 23:7-8, he looks forward to the day when the people will not look for an example of the Lord's power from the return from Egypt, but rather from a future return from the land of the north (Babylon).

The second exodus theme has as its foundation the curses of the Mosaic covenant. God brought them out of the land of Egypt through an act of his grace. He then gave them the law on Mount Sinai which included the curses for disobedience. The final curse actually describes their punishment as a return to enslavement in Egypt: "Then the Lord will send you back to Egypt in ships, to a destination I promised you would never see again. There you will offer yourselves to your enemies as slaves, but no one will buy you" (Deut 28:68). The prophetic judgments are thus styled as returns to Egypt and their salvation oracles thus use Exodus language to describe restoration.

ANTICIPATORY FULFILLMENTS IN THE POSTEXILIC PERIOD

The prophetic expectation of divine judgment was fulfilled in the removal of northern Israel and its incorporation into the Assyrian empire and the exile of many leading Judeans to Babylon beginning in 586 B.C.

This period of punishment lasted until 539 B.C. when Cyrus of Persia defeated the Babylonians and allowed many if not all of Babylon's vassals to return to their lands and rebuild their temples.

Ezra 1–6 recounts the early returns under such leaders as Sheshbazzar and Zerubbabel. Those who heard the prophetic message would have understood the exile as a reversion to bondage and a wandering in the wilderness. Thus, we should not be surprised that the faithful would think of the return to the land as a fulfillment of the promises of the second exodus.

Throntveit perceptively points out parallels in the book of Ezra's account of the return from exile and the exodus.[1] For instance, it is striking that just as the Egyptians gave gifts to the departing children of Israel (Ex 3:21-22; 11:2; 12:35-36), so did Israel's present foreign neighbors: "And all their neighbors assisted by giving them articles of silver and gold, supplies for the journey and livestock. They gave them many valuable gifts in addition to all the voluntary offerings" (Ezra 1:6). As the Exodus generation gave gifts to the construction of the tabernacle (Ex 35:21-29), so the returnees contributed gifts to the construction of the temple (Ezra 2:68-69).

It is undeniable that the return from exile was seen as a fulfillment of the expectation of the second exodus. However, as we read on in the Christian canon, we see that more was yet to come.

JESUS CHRIST: THE ULTIMATE FULFILLMENT OF THE EXODUS

The Gospel story begins in the wilderness. Mark cites Isaiah 40:3[2] at the head of his account of Jesus' ministry (Mk 1:2-3):

Look, I am sending my messenger ahead of you,
and he will prepare your way.
He is a voice shouting in the wilderness,
"Prepare the way for the LORD's coming!
Clear the road for him!"

---

[1]See M. Throntveit, *Ezra-Nehemiah* (Louisville: Westminster John Knox, 1999), pp. 15-18.

[2]In the Greek version and in connection with Malachi 3:1.

After this announcement, the narrative turns to John the Baptist, who is preaching and baptizing people in the wilderness. The story of Jesus' life that follows is permeated with allusions to the exodus and wilderness wanderings. The following rehearsal of the story will combine readings from all the gospels, though arguably Matthew, the gospel that seems directed particularly toward Christians of Jewish origins, seems to make the most of the connections between the Lord and the time of the exodus.

Jesus' ministry begins with his baptism, a passing through the waters, reminiscent of the *Yam Suf* (the Re[e]d Sea, see discussion on pp. 113-14) crossing. After all, Paul, likely reflecting first century A.D. Jewish theological ideas, speaks of the Israelites' crossing of the *Yam Suf* as their baptism:

> *I don't want you to forget, dear brothers and sisters, about our ancestors in the wilderness long ago. All of them were guided by a cloud that moved ahead of them, and all of them walked through the sea on dry ground. In the cloud and in the sea, all of them were baptized as followers of Moses. (1 Cor 10:1-3).*

The connection between Jesus' baptism and the crossing of the sea is accentuated by the fact that the former is followed by 40 days and 40 nights in the wilderness, just as Israel spent 40 years in the wilderness.

The connection between the 40 years and the 40 days and nights in the wilderness goes much deeper than a mere number. The temptations that Jesus experienced in the wilderness are the same as those of Israel. The difference between the two is that Jesus was obedient where Israel was disobedient.

First temptation. Jesus had been fasting for many days and certainly was famished. The devil advises him to turn the stones into loaves of bread but Jesus refuses, citing Deuteronomy 8:3: "People do not live by bread alone, but by every word that comes from the mouth of God." The significance of the citation from Deuteronomy is that this Old Testament book contains Moses' final sermon to the Israelites, exhorting the second generation about to enter the Promised Land not to disobey as their fathers had disobeyed in the wilderness. Jesus is the obedient son of God in contrast to Israel, God's disobedient sons.

Second temptation. The devil now takes Jesus to the highest point of the temple and tells him to throw himself off. God will show his love and care for him by sending angels to catch him. Again, Jesus responds by citing Deuteronomy: "You must not test the LORD your God" (Deut 6:16). Jesus' obedience again contrasts with the disobedience of Israel in the wilderness where they constantly tested God.

Third temptation. Finally the devil tells Jesus to bend the knee to him and in return he will give Jesus all the kingdoms of the world. The Israelites had bent the knee to a false god, the Golden Calf (Ex 32), but Jesus refuses and for a final time cites Deuteronomy: "You must worship the LORD your God and serve only him" (Deut 6:13).

After demonstrating that he is God's obedient son (in contrast to Israel), Jesus now chooses the disciples, twelve in all. The number, of course, is deliberate and reflects the twelve tribes of Israel. Jesus is forming a new people of God.

Perhaps one of the most well-known portions of the Gospel of Matthew is the Sermon on the Mount (Mt 5–7), so-called because Jesus delivers his message from a mountainside (Mt 5:1). The topic of the Sermon is the law. A reader versed in the Old Testament cannot fail to miss the parallel with Mount Sinai. In the Old Testament God delivers the law from the top of a mountain and now Jesus speaks about the law from a mountaintop. That Matthew is particularly interested in drawing these parallels is highlighted by noting that the same sermon in Luke is reported to have taken place on a plain (Lk 6:17). Harmonizations are possible but can distract from the theological significance of Matthew's placement of the sermon on a mountain.

Luke 9:31 reports the topic of conversation between Jesus, Moses and Elijah at the Mount of Transfiguration. The NLT translation of the verse brings it out most clearly when it renders "they were speaking about his exodus from this world, which was about to be fulfilled in Jerusalem."

These parallels between Jesus' ministry and the experiences of the exodus generation are just a sampling. The culmination takes place at the end of his life when he is crucified on the eve of the Passover (Mt 26;

Mk 14; Lk 22), the annual celebration of the exodus from Egypt. After all, Jesus is our Passover Lamb (1 Cor 5:7). He is the fulfillment of the exodus. The exodus is an anticipation of the even greater redemptive act of God in Jesus' death and resurrection.

LIVING THE EXODUS

The book of Hebrews uses the exodus and wilderness wandering tradition in a different way. Psalm 95:7d-11 encourages its readers to obey God based on the sad experience of the exodus generation when it left Egypt. God saved them from their bondage, but they never entered the Promised Land because they disobeyed God. They died in the wilderness; their corpses rotted there. The author of Hebrews (Heb 3:1–4:13) cites the psalm and applies it to Christian readers. They have been saved by Jesus, but they have not yet entered the rest of their Promised Land (heaven). To enter that rest, they must remain faithful to God or like their ancient predecessors, they will die and not enter their reward.

LIBERATION THEOLOGY

The exodus is the account of God freeing Israel from their Egyptian bondage. Some theologians and biblical scholars have evoked the exodus to suggest that God is on the side of the poor and the oppressed. The exodus thus becomes a message of hope for them. Pixley and Boff claim that "Yahweh, the God of the Bible, is characterized by his preferential option for the oppressed."[3] Kirk-Duggan reads the exodus story as "unfolding a divine preference for the persecuted, the disempowered as a mode to expose, dialogue about, and then eliminate classism, sexism, racism, anti-Semitism, homophobia and other experiences of oppression."[4]

However, such a reading and application of the exodus is out of keeping with the biblical text. Exodus links Yahweh's actions toward Israel not in

---

[3]See G. V. Pixley and C. Boff, "A Latin American Perspective: The Option for the Poor in the Old Testament," in *Voices from the Margin: Interpreting the Bible in the Third World*, ed. R. S. Sugirtharajah (Maryknoll, N.Y.: Orbis, 2006), p. 209.

[4]C. A. Kirk-Duggan, "Let My People Go! Threads of Exodus in African American Narratives," in *Voices from the Margin*, p. 259.

the fact that they are oppressed, pure and simple, but in the promises made to the patriarchs, promises that were not given to all the poor of the world. Indeed, to make their thesis work, Pixley and Boff have to argue that sixth-century priests changed the text of Exodus in a way that obscured, but did not totally efface, Yahweh's preferential treatment of the poor as oppressed and not as recipients of the patriarchal promises.[5] Even if this speculative recreation of the redaction of Exodus were true, however, the canonical book of Exodus is the final form, not some hypothetical earlier form.

In the final analysis, though one should not doubt Yahweh's concern for the suffering of any human being (Exodus and much of the Bible critiques those who exploit men and women created in the image of God), the exodus story is not the guarantee of political and economic liberation for anyone.[6] It anticipates the greater liberation to be found in Jesus Christ culminating, as nineteenth-century African American writing and hymns put it so powerfully, in our crossing the Jordan into the promised land of heaven.[7]

QUESTIONS FOR DISCUSSION

1. As you think about the New Testament's message, can you see other connections to the exodus theme beyond those pointed out in this chapter?

2. How does thinking of yourself as one who has experienced the exodus but not yet come into your Promised Land affect how you think about yourself and how you act?

---

[5]Pixley and Boff, "Latin American Perspective," p. 214.

[6]Furthermore, as we saw in chapter three, the exodus is really not a move from bondage to freedom, but rather from bondage to an oppressive king to bondage to the true king, Yahweh. While liberation theology uses the exodus theme to further release from oppression it rarely emphasizes the requirement to serve the divine King.

[7]In writing about liberation theology, C. Padilla says "God does not merely 'act in history,' God acts in history in particular ways. It would be a denial of the history to separate an abstract project label like liberation from the specific meaning of the liberation God has brought," "Liberation Theology," in *Freedom and Discipleship* (Maryknoll, N.Y.: Orbis, 1989), quoted in S. Escobar, "Liberation Theologies and Hermeneutics," in *Dictionary for Theological Interpretation of the Bible*, ed. Kevin J. Vanhoozer (Grand Rapids: Baker, 2005), p. 455.

3. Do you think the analogy between Christ and the Old Testament exodus is simply a matter of coincidence or perhaps a conscious shaping of Jesus' life to conform to the exodus, or is God shaping events so that the exodus foreshadows the work of Christ?

4. In this chapter, we observed and criticized the use of the exodus as a paradigm of God delivering the poor and exploited from their oppressors. What are your thoughts about liberation theology?

FOR FURTHER READING

Schipani, D., ed. *Freedom and Discipleship.* Maryknoll, N.Y.: Orbis, 1989.
Stock, Augustine. *The Way in the Wilderness.* Collegeville, Minn.: Liturgical Press, 1969.
Watts, R. E. *Isaiah's New Exodus in Mark.* Grand Rapids: Baker, 2001.

ELEVEN

THE ROLE OF LAW
IN THE CHRISTIAN LIFE

The second section of Exodus presents the Book of the Covenant (Ex 19–24), the oldest law collection in the Pentateuch. While many Christians believe that the difference between the Old and New Testaments may be described as the difference between law and grace, we have already observed (chapter 7) that the Old Testament law was given within the context of grace.

However, few would argue that Christians observe the Old Testament law in its fullness.[1] Not many Christians, for example, are concerned to observe the final law of the law collection, "You must not cook a young goat in its mother's milk" (Ex 23:19). On the other hand, not many Christians would say that there is no divine law that is relevant for today. After all, murder, proscribed by the sixth commandment, is universally recognized as wrong by Christians, even though what constitutes murder may be debated.

---

[1]Though writers commonly labeled "theonomists" come very close to doing so. See, for example, R. J. Rushdoony, *The Institutes of Biblical Law* (Phillipsburg, N.J.: P & R, 1973), and G. L. Bahnsen, *Theonomy in Christian Ethics* (Nutley, N.J.: Craig Publishing, 1977), and the critique offered by the faculty of Westminster Theological Seminary in W. S. Barker and W. Robert Godfrey, eds., *Theonomy: A Reformed Critique* (Grand Rapids: Zondervan, 1990).

What makes one Old Testament law relevant and another irrelevant? Are there principles involved or is it simply a matter of modern taste?

THE CASE LAW AND ITS PENALTIES TODAY

How do the laws of Exodus apply to us today? They come from an ancient Near Eastern society and we live in a modern Western society. Do the laws have any relevance for us?

The New Testament affirms that the law continues to apply today. Indeed, Jesus famously said that "until heaven and earth disappear, not even the smallest detail of God's law will disappear until its purpose is achieved" (Mt 5:18).

With one exception (the Sabbath), few doubt the continuing significance of the Ten Commandments. The New Testament affirms that sole and proper worship of the true God, honor toward one's parents, and the prohibition of murder, adultery, theft, lying and coveting remain requirements for those who want to please God.

On the other hand, few believe that the case law still applies. What would it mean to refrain from cooking a young goat in its mother's milk (Ex 23:19b)?

Above it was shown that the case laws are applications of the principles of the Ten Commandments to the specific social and redemptive-historical situation of the people of God. Christians live in a different social and redemptive-historical moment.

For instance, because we live in the time period after Jesus came and died, we no longer celebrate the three annual festivals that commemorated Old Testament redemptive events and anticipated the coming of Christ (Ex 23:14-18). Indeed, all the laws associated with Israelite ritual as well as those that distanced Israel from Canaanite ritual (including Ex 23:19b) are no longer observed. Thus, the altar law of 20:24-26 is not relevant to modern Western society. We don't build altars today and the prohibition not to have stairs at an altar is doubly irrelevant because that was a law that meant to keep Israel from mimicking Canaanite sexual practices or even the hint of them during their own sacred observances, an issue no longer relevant.

Even so, such laws can provide guidance to Christians today as we seek to apply the Ten Commandments to our social and redemptive-historical situations. The goring-ox law, for instance, can warn us that those who commit negligent homicide are responsible for their actions. In rural settings, this could still apply to a goring ox. In an inner city context, it could apply to dangerous pit bulls. It could also apply to damage done by a driver who knows their car's brakes are faulty. The laws that keep Israel from acting like Canaanites in worship (the altar law and the law prohibiting cooking a young goat in its mother's milk) warn Christians about the danger of importing the practices of false religions into our own worship.

The relevance of the penalties of the law is more difficult to assess. Here the important fact to keep in mind is that in the Old Testament the law was directed to God's people when they had the form of a nation state. As a nation state, God's people were to remain pure and therefore penalties had a physical nature. Serious criminals had to be removed physically.

On the other hand, God's people today have a spiritual form. The church is drawn from many nations and its weapons are not physical but spiritual. Recurrent and unrepentant sinners should not be executed by the church, but they should be excommunicated. In this way, the covenant community remains pure.

THE PRINCIPLE OF CONTINUING RELEVANCE

Above, we have suggested that the Ten Commandments provide ethical principles that are applied to specific situations in the case law. The case law thus is directly relevant to Israel, but may not continue to be relevant as a guide to God's will for his people in the twenty-first century A.D.

The ceremonial law. Modern theologians have long divided the law into three categories: the moral, civil and ceremonial law.[2] Moral laws

---

[2]Though Christopher J. H. Wright, *Old Testament Ethics for the People of God* (Downers Grove, Ill.: InterVarsity Press, 2004), p. 288, is an example of a theologian who rejects this distinction as anachronistic.

are laws that regulate human conduct. Many of the case laws can be classified as moral: "Kidnappers must be put to death, whether they are caught in possession of their victims or have already sold them as slaves" (an application of the commandment not to steal). Other case laws are civil laws that regulate the government of Israel. We have not and will not dwell long on civil law because the Book of the Covenant has no examples, while Deuteronomy has many of them (see the law concerning kingship in Deut 17:14-20). The Book of the Covenant has a number of laws that may be categorized as ceremonial (or ritual) law. These are laws that pertain to the formal worship of Israel. They emanate from the first four commandments (though the first three are not ceremonial laws themselves [see below on the Sabbath]). Ceremonial laws are found in 20:22-26 and also in the laws establishing the three annual festivals (Unleavened Bread, Harvest, and Final Harvest) in 23:14-17, to which are appended laws concerning sacrifice and offerings (Ex 23:18-19).

It has often been pointed out that the Israelites themselves did not differentiate their laws into these three categories. That is true enough. We observe no attempt to group laws in this way; examples of all three categories are often mixed together. However, to go further and to suggest that the categorization is therefore illegitimate is misguided. From our later vantage point, we can see that certain laws that were associated with ritual were fulfilled by Christ and are no longer actively observed. Since Christ is the once-and-for-all sacrifice, we no longer offer sacrifices. Since Christ is the very presence of God and after his ascension to heaven the Holy Spirit was sent, we no longer need to build tabernacles or temples (or construct altars). Though laws concerning priesthood are not found in the Book of the Covenant (but they are in Lev 8:10-20), we can see that the same is true concerning the priesthood, which institution Jesus fulfilled. Finally, and relevant for Exodus, Jesus also fulfilled ceremonial time. Thus, we no longer observe the annual festivals . . . or the Sabbath. And here we have an enigma which disturbs the simplicity of the general principle that we stated above.

THE SABBATH: A COMMANDMENT
NO LONGER OBSERVED

As we survey the New Testament, I think it is fair to say that nine of the commandments continue to be in effect. Worshiping other gods, making idols, misusing God's name, dishonoring parents, murder, committing adultery, theft, lying and coveting do not become virtues or irrelevant actions with the coming of Christ. To sin in these ways would be a betrayal of one's commitment to Christ ("Everyone who sins is breaking God's law, for all sin is contrary to the law of God. . . . Anyone who keeps on sinning does not know him or understand who he is," 1 Jn 3:4, 6).

But note Paul's argument in Colossians 2:16-17: "So don't let anyone condemn you for what you eat or drink, or for not celebrating certain holy days or new moon ceremonies or Sabbaths. For these rules are only shadows of the reality yet to come. And Christ himself is that reality." Paul believes that the commandment to observe the Sabbath is no longer binding on the conscience of the Christian.

While this is not the place to enter into a full discussion of the issue,[3] it appears that the Sabbath law should be considered a ceremonial law within the Ten Commandments and therefore a law deeply affected by the coming of Christ, who fulfilled Israel's ritual, showing that it was the shadow of the reality—Christ himself.

Thus, we do not observe the Sabbath as they did during the Old Testament time period. It is not a matter of legal obligation not to work on the Sabbath. There is, however, a principle here that one needs to bear in mind. God created us with bodies and minds that need periodic rest. No one can work twenty-four hours a day, seven days a week, or even eight hours a day, seven days a week and not have diminishing returns on their labor. It is a matter of wisdom to observe a rest periodically. More than that, though, we should gather together to worship God. Individual worship is fine and good, but we need our fellow believers to support and encourage us. The book of Hebrews tells Christians to "not

---

[3]Though see my full discussion in *Immanuel in Our Place* (Phillipsburg, N.J.: P & R, 2001), pp. 161-84.

neglect our meeting together, as some people do, but encourage one another" (Heb 10:25). Again, it is a matter of wisdom to pick a day out of the week to rest from our regular labors and to come together to worship. Whether someone then goes out to eat, plays tennis, watches football, enjoys time with friends, even does a little work, is a matter of individual conscience.

CONCLUSION
While God is unchangeable, his law is not always the same from generation to generation. The changes are not because God is fickle in what he wants, but rather because his people change over time and because his work of redemption progresses from age to age. Christians need to use their sanctified intelligence and Christ-transformed conscience as well as a well-informed hermeneutic as they seek God's will in the law.

QUESTIONS FOR DISCUSSION
Read through the case laws of the Book of the Covenant section by section (use the outline listed below[4]) and ask yourself what these laws meant in their Old Testament context. Reflect on whether these laws retain relevance and in what way in the present.

Altar Laws	*20:22-24*
Slave Laws	*21:1-11*
Personal Injury Laws	*21:12-36*
Property Laws	*22:1-15*
Interpersonal Laws	*22:16-31*
Miscellaneous Laws	*23:1-13*
Ceremonial Laws	*23:14-19*

FOR FURTHER READING
Barker, W. S., and W. R. Godfrey, eds. *Theonomy: A Reformed Critique.* Grand Rapids: Zondervan, 1990.

---

[4]The categories of the list are imperfect since there is not a strict categorization of laws in these ancient collections.

Longman, Tremper, III. *Immanuel in Our Place: Seeing Christ in Israel's Worship.* Phillipsburg, N.J.: P & R, 2001.

Wright, Christopher J. H. *Old Testament Ethics for the People of God.* Downers Grove, Ill.: InterVarsity Press, 2004.

TWELVE

THE WORD BECAME FLESH
AND TABERNACLED AMONG US

The tabernacle was a symbol of God's presence on earth (see chapter 8). Yes, it was a tent—an ornate tent, but a tent nonetheless. However, this tent was God's tent among the tents of his people. In this way, he let them know he was with them as they traveled up from Egypt. He was one of them, but he was far superior to them. His tent was the tent of the war leader, the king, located in the center of the camp. No one should approach this tent unprepared or they would meet a horrific fate. Approaching it with respect and an acknowledgement of sin and subservience, however, led to blessing and a good relationship with God. The tent with the deep blue curtain serving as its ceiling symbolically pointed to heaven. Other symbolism of the tabernacle, including the lampstand ornamented like an almond tree, pointed to Eden where God lived in harmony with his human creatures.

The tabernacle, whose description encompasses almost half of the book of Exodus, was thus an incredibly significant structure. However, it was not the first or the last representation of the presence of God on earth. From Genesis to Revelation God makes himself known among his people. The tabernacle was appropriate for its redemptive moment, but it replaced altars and was itself replaced by the temple.

This chapter rehearses the biblical theology of the presence of God. How does God make himself known among his people? How does a perfect, holy, transcendent, yet immanent deity reveal himself to an imperfect, sinful, earth-bound creature? The story does begin in the Garden of Eden.

BEFORE THE TABERNACLE

The Garden of Eden (Gen 2–3). God created Adam and Eve in his image and in perfect relationship with himself.[1] God walked in the Garden with his human creatures.[2] Of course, God did not have legs and literally walk with Adam and Eve, but the metaphor expresses the companionship and harmonious relationship that existed between them. The Garden was a place where Adam and Eve could meet with God any place. No specific place had to be set apart for meeting with God, because every place was appropriate—that is, until the Fall.

In the middle of the Garden was a tree, the tree of the knowledge of good and evil. God warned Adam not to eat the fruit of this tree. According to the text (Gen 2:17), God gave no explanation for this prohibition, but announced that if they ate the fruit they would die.

The tree was a test concerning human obedience to divine command. Would Adam and Eve submit to God's requirement, even if there were no further explanation? Would they allow God to define what was right and wrong or would they usurp the Creator's prerogative and arrogate to themselves the power to define morality? The answer is well known. They ate from the fruit; they rebelled against God.

Sin changed everything. A holy God does not tolerate sin. Sin created a barrier between God and Adam and Eve. No longer could they stay in Eden. God expelled them, ending an easy relationship. From that point on, humans met God in special locations. These special locations often

---

[1]See Longman, *How to Read Genesis* (Downers Grove, Ill.: InterVarsity Press, 2005), p. 102-9.

[2]Though this is not stated until Gen 3:8, it seems reasonable to think that this was God's common custom before the Fall.

had echoes of the Eden of the past and anticipated the restoration of Eden in the future.

Simple altars (from Adam and Eve to Moses). After Adam and Eve's treachery, God could have justly finished his relationship with his human creatures, but he didn't. Rather, in the midst of punishing them, he announced his intention to stay involved with them and work toward their restoration. In his judgment speech against the serpent, God stated: "And I will cause hostility between you and the woman, and between your offspring and her offspring. He will strike your head, and you will strike his heel" (Gen 3:15). Further, he gives them a token of his continued involvement by giving them animal skins as clothing (Gen 3:21).

Even so, humans had to acknowledge their sin as they approached their holy God. They could no longer meet God in fellowship just anywhere; a special place had to be set apart for fellowship with him. In Hebrew, the verb which communicates the act of setting something or someone apart is *qdsh,* which can also be translated "to be holy" or "consecrated."[3]

Upon expulsion from the Garden, that sacred space was associated with an altar, a translation of the Hebrew word *mizbeah.* This noun is formed from a verb *zbh,* which means "to sacrifice" and points to its nature as a place of sacrifice. The first mention of an altar does not come until Genesis 8:20. In the aftermath of the flood, "Noah built an altar to the LORD, and there he sacrificed as burnt offerings the animals and birds that had been approved for that purpose."[4] The connection between altar and sacrifice is here explicit and we can safely assume that when altars are mentioned that sacrifice was part of the ritual practiced there. After all, as part of the process of sinful humans' approach to God, they have to make an acknowledgement of their sin and the fact that they deserved to die for their sins. Sacrifice, as we later hear explicitly in Leviticus 1–7, functions in large part to serve as a substitute for

---

[3]See J. A. Naudé, *"qdsh,"* in *New International Dictionary of Old Testament Theology and Exegesis,* ed. Willem VanGemeren (Grand Rapids: Zondervan, 1997), 3:877-87.

[4]NLT; more literally, the sacrificial animals are described as "every clean animal and every clean bird."

human sin and symbolically achieves atonement with God.[5]

Though Noah's altar is the first one mentioned by name, we should probably assume the presence of altars as early as the time of Adam and Eve. If sacrifice may be implied by the presence of an altar, the presence of an altar may be implied by the act of sacrifice. In Genesis 4 we have the story of Cain and Abel's sacrifice. Though an altar is not mentioned, we presume that they brought their sacrifices to such a place.

Altars become a more common part of the narrative in the account of the patriarchs, particularly the Abraham story. Upon traveling to the Promised Land, Abraham wanders the land that is not yet his, but is promised to his descendants. The narrative makes a point of his construction of altars at various places in the land. He builds an altar at Shechem in the north, his first recorded stopping area (Gen 12:7). Consequently, he erects altars at a location between Bethel and Ai (Gen 12:8; 13:4), in Hebron (Gen 13:18), and on a mountain in the region of Moriah (Gen 22:9). His grandson Jacob also builds an altar at Bethel (Gen 35:1-7). One gets the feeling that the patriarchs are in essence planting flags of God's presence all through the Promised Land.

But what did an altar look like during this period? We probably get the best picture from a law from the Book of the Covenant. This law presupposes the construction of multiple altars (a practice that will stop once the law of centralization [Deut 12] goes into effect [see below]):

> Build for me an altar made of earth, and offer your sacrifices to me—your burnt offerings and peace offerings, your sheep and goats, and your cattle. Build my altar wherever I cause my name to be remembered, and I will come to you and bless you. If you use stones to build my altar, use only natural, uncut stones. Do not shape the stones with a tool, for that would make the altar unfit for holy use. And do not approach my altar by going up steps. If you do, someone might look up under your clothing and see your nakedness. (Ex 20:24-26)

The construction is simple, the location small, in keeping with the period of redemptive history where the people of God are an extended family and the head of the family led the religious rituals.

---

[5]See Longman, *Immanuel in Our Place*, pp. 75-101.

THE TABERNACLE

As time progressed and the patriarchal period gave way to the period of Moses, a simple altar would no longer suffice, nor would the patriarch acting as a priest figure. And here we have caught up with the period that is the main subject of this book. Thus, chapter nine explored the structure and significance of the tabernacle, a large corporate worship center that included a sacrificial altar and was serviced by a class of newly ordained priests.

The tabernacle is appropriate for the new social situation of the people of God. They are no longer simply a large family, but a significantly-sized group in the process of achieving nation status. However, during the period that the tabernacle is operative Israel has not yet firmly nor completely established itself in the land. Thus, while the people live in tents, God lives in a tent. While this is obvious during the period of the forty years of wilderness wandering, it is also true in the period between the entry into the land and the time of David, as we will make clear in the next section where the tabernacle gives way to the temple.

THE TEMPLE

The transition from tabernacle to temple begins with David. In 2 Samuel 7, David informs the prophet Nathan of his intention to build God a "house" *(bayit)*. After all, he lived in a beautiful cedar house, so why should God continue to make his earthly presence known in the form of a tent?

Nathan's first reaction was positive, but that evening God informed him in no uncertain terms that David's plan was faulty. Who was David to suggest such a thing? As we observed in connection with the tabernacle, the building of the holy place was always a result of divine initiative and plan.

So David would not build the "house" for God. Rather God would build a "house" for David. Of course, this "house" was a dynasty of kings, and at that time God established a covenant with David that established that his descendants would occupy the throne in Jerusalem.

Of greater significance for our present topic, God also announces that his house will be built in the future by David's "own offspring." The book of Chronicles in particular narrates David's extensive preparations for the work of his son.

Why wasn't it appropriate for David to build the temple, when it was for his son Solomon? David himself gives the answer to Solomon:

> *"My son, I wanted to build a Temple to honor the name of the* LORD *my God,"* David *told him. "But the* LORD *said to me, 'You have killed many men in the battles you have fought. And since you have shed so much blood in my sight, you will not be the one to build a Temple to honor my name. But you will have a son who will be a man of peace. I will give him peace with his enemies in all the surrounding lands. His name will be Solomon, and I will give peace and quiet to Israel during his reign. (2 Chron 22:7-9)*

What was it about David's shedding blood that disqualified him? Many readers wrongly believe this is a moral judgment against David, but that is hard to believe since it was God himself who ordered David into holy war for God's own glory. No, the disqualification is not a moral one, but a redemptive-historical statement. The temple represented stability and establishment in the land. David was the one who completed the conquest by defeating the final internal enemies (particularly the Philistines), and he would turn over a stable kingdom to his son, Solomon, whose very name when translated into English means "Peace" (his name is related to the well-known Hebrew word *shalom*).

Associated with the move from the mobile tent sanctuary (the tabernacle) to the firmly rooted temple is the law of centralization of Deuteronomy 12. God through Moses announced that Israel was to worship him in one and only one place, the place that he chose. In other words, God's people could only offer sacrifice at one location. There would be only one sacrificial altar and it would not move.

Some conclude that such a requirement is at odds with the law just cited in Exodus 20:24-26, which implies the construction of multiple altars. However, they ignore the fact that the Deuteronomic requirement did not go into effect until they "drive out the nations that live there." As we have just discussed, David was the one who accomplished this, finishing the conquest—now was the time for temple construction. Israel was established in the land of promise.

In many ways, the temple continued the symbolic significance of the tabernacle (see chapter nine). God made his presence known in the midst of his people by this "house." For instance, just as the tree-like menorah alluded to Eden, so did the extensive garden ornaments associated with the temple as can be observed even in the passages quoted in the next couple of paragraphs.

The architectural innovations, though, symbolized the fact of establishment. Of course, this is obvious in the very structure of a house as opposed to a tent. But other features support this. Note for instance the description of the two pillars:

> *Huram cast two bronze pillars, each 27 feet tall and 18 feet in circumference. For the tops of the pillars he cast bronze capitals, each 7 ½ feet tall. Each capital was decorated with seven sets of latticework and interwoven chains. He also encircled the latticework with two rows of pomegranates to decorate the capitals over the pillars. . . . The capitals on the two pillars had 200 pomegranates in two rows around them. . . . He named the one on the south Jakin, and the one on the north Boaz. The capitals on the pillars were shaped like water lilies.* (1 Kings 7:15-22)

These pillars, and notice the garden (of Eden) imagery, represented stability, establishment, firmness. Even their names, Jakin ("he will establish") and Boaz ("by strength"), strengthen this association.

Another innovation was a large laver of water, likely used for priestly lustration rites:

> *Then Huram cast a great round basin, 15 feet across from rim to rim, called the Sea. It was 7 ½ feet deep and about 45 feet in circumference. It was encircled just below its rim by two rows of decorative gourds. There were about six gourds per foot all the way around and they were cast as part of the basin.* (1 Kings 7:23-24)

Notice the name of this basin of water—Sea, in Hebrew, *Yam*. The sea in the Old Testament often connotes forces of chaos that threaten to overwhelm creation order. This idea comes from ancient Near Eastern mythology where the God of creation fought the Sea and then controlled the waters to bring about the land. Indeed, in the Canaanite myth, the god's name was Yam. Here, though, Yam is controlled, limited to a basin of water. The forces of chaos (the Canaanites) have been quelled. God is in control.

Solomon constructed the temple in the tenth century B.C., but its history was a sad one. Solomon himself and most of his descendants betrayed the relationship they had with God. One of the forms that this betrayal took was the religious pollution of the temple. Many of these kings allowed pagan symbols to be placed in the Holy of Holies. Even so, the people treated the temple with presumption. Jeremiah warned against this in his famous temple sermon (Jer 7). They sinned and scoffed at the prophet's warnings to them of coming judgment because, after all, the temple was in the city. God would not let anything happen to his house!

But they were wrong. God abandoned his temple (Ezek 9–11). He then raised up the Babylonians (Hab 1:6) to destroy the temple in 586 B.C. Lamentations 2 bemoans the destruction of this house.

Though God judged his people, he was not done with them. After the exile, they returned and rebuilt the temple (Ezra 1–6) under the leadership of Zerubbabel and the instigation of the prophets Haggai and Zechariah. The second temple was finished in 515 B.C. and it lasted until the time of Jesus.

JESUS, THE PRESENCE OF GOD

According to Haggai, the physical splendor of the second temple was no match for the first temple. However, before Jesus began his earthly ministry, Herod the Great had expanded and aggrandized the temple into something magnificent.

Jesus honored and respected the temple. As a young man, his parents took him to the temple, where he stayed behind and confounded the wise men. When his worried parents found him there, he responded to their concern with "Didn't you know that I must be in my Father's house?" (Lk 2:49). "Zeal for his Father's house" led him to rid the temple area of the moneychangers (Jn 2:17, citing Ps 69:9).

Even so, he knew that this building was temporary. It foreshadowed something greater. It represented God's presence. Jesus himself made God's presence known, thus rendering the temple obsolete. The prologue to John says as much:

> *In the beginning the Word already existed.*
> *The Word was with God,*
> *and the Word was God. . . .*
> *So the Word became human and made his home among us.* (Jn 1:1, 14)

The verb rendered "made his home" in verse 14 has special significance to our theme. The Greek root of the verb (*skēnoō*) is related to a noun that means "tabernacle" (*skēnē*). In other words, Jesus tabernacled among his people.

Jesus' presence on earth signaled a tremendous change in the concept of sacred space. He anticipated this change in his conversation with the Samaritan woman at the well (Jn 4). Samaritans were not true Jewish people, but the result of the influx of foreign people into the northern part of the kingdom after the Assyrians defeated the Israelites in 722 B.C. They had a hybrid form of worship and the Samaritan woman expressed the difference in her comments to Jesus: "Why is it that you Jews insist that Jerusalem is the only place of worship, while we Samaritans claim it is here at Mount Gerizim, where our ancestors worshiped?" (Jn 4:20). In Jesus' response we come to understand that a dramatic change is coming: "Believe me, dear woman, the time is coming when it will no longer matter whether you worship the Father on this mountain or in Jerusalem. You Samaritans know very little about the one you worship, while we Jews know all about him, for salvation comes through the Jews. But the time is coming—indeed it's here now—when true worshipers will worship the Father in sprit and in truth" (Jn 4:21-23).

Toward the end of his earthly career, Jesus' words become even more provocative about the future of the temple. Mark 13 (see parallel accounts in Mt 24 and Lk 21) recounts a time when the disciples stood amazed at the grandeur of the temple and the size of the stones. Jesus replied "Yes, look at these great buildings. But they will be completely demolished. Not one stone will be left on top of another" (Mk 13:2).

Earlier, after driving out the moneychangers, Jesus told the Jewish leaders that if the temple were destroyed "in three days I will raise it up" (Jn
2:19). The Gospel goes on to say that by "'this temple,' he meant his own
body" (Jn 2:21). Soon after the conversation recorded in Mark 13 he
found himself before Caiaphas the high priest accused of saying that he
would destroy the temple and raise it up in three days (Mk 14:58).

Jesus was associating himself with the temple, the three days being
an obvious reference to his future resurrection. Jesus is the fulfillment
of the temple. He is the very presence of God. His death and resurrection meant that the distinction between holy and common space was
eradicated. Now every place was holy, that is, every place is a place
where people can have intimate fellowship with God through Jesus
Christ. It is not surprising, then, that at the moment of his death, the
veil that separated the Holy of Holies from the rest of the temple area
was split in two (Mt 27:51). A few years later (70 A.D.) the temple itself
was destroyed and not rebuilt.

Now of course not everyone can be in the physical presence of Jesus,
and no one can since his death. However, once he ascended to heaven he
sent the Holy Spirit which fills the church and the individual believer.
Indeed, many New Testament passages make an analogy between the
temple which was filled with the Glory of God and the church or Christian who are filled with the Holy Spirit.

Paul says as much concerning the church in Ephesians 2:19-22:

> So now you Gentiles are no longer strangers and foreigners. You are citizens
> along with all of God's holy people. You are members of God's family. To-
> gether, we are his house, built on the foundation of the apostles and the proph-
> ets. And the cornerstone is Christ Jesus himself. We are carefully joined to-
> gether in him, becoming a holy temple for the Lord. Through him you Gentiles
> are also being made part of this dwelling where God lives by his Spirit.

Paul also understands that the Holy Spirit's presence in believers renders them mini-temples, a fact that has serious ethical implications according to 2 Corinthians 6:14-16:

> Don't team up with those who are unbelievers. How can righteousness be a

partner with wickedness? How can light live with darkness? What harmony can there be between Christ and the devil? How can a believer be a partner with an unbeliever? And what union can there be between God's temple and idols? For we are the Temple of the living God.

And then in another place (1 Cor 6:18-20) the apostle warns:

Run from sexual sin! No other sin so clearly affects the body as this one does. For sexual immorality is a sin against your own body. Don't you realize that your body is the temple of the Holy Spirit, who lives in you and was given to you by God? You do not belong to yourself, for God bought you with a high price. So you must honor God with your body.

In short, then, with the coming of Jesus the relevance of a special place to meet with God has faded away. No longer and never again will there be a divinely sanctioned holy site. After all, now every place is holy. The believer can call on the name of God anywhere. The Holy Spirit dwells not in an architectural structure but in the church and in the individual believer's heart.

THE NEW JERUSALEM

At the conclusion of redemptive history comes the consummation. God brings his people back into a harmonious relationship with himself. Revelation 21–22 uses the image of the New Jerusalem to describe what we would also call heaven. It is a highly symbolic description, two features of which are particularly important for our theme.

In the first place, the description goes out of its way not only to tell us what was in the New Jerusalem, but what wasn't. John is struck by the absence of the temple. "I saw no temple in the city" (Rev 21:22). Since God's presence permeates the whole city, there was no need for a temple. The verse goes on to say as much: "for the Lord God Almighty and the Lamb are its temple."

In the second place, the New Jerusalem has a river running through it. It was "a river with the water of life, clear as crystal, flowing from the throne of God and of the Lamb. It flowed down the center of the main street" (Rev 22:1-2a). Revelation 22:2b goes on to say that on each side of the river was a "tree of life."

In other words, we are back to Eden! Two trees of life show we are not only restored to Eden, but we are in something that in some way even supersedes Eden.

SUMMARY

The tabernacle is not an isolated concept in the Bible, but fits into a biblical theology of God's presence that flows from the first chapters of Genesis to the concluding chapters of Revelation.

Eden → altars → tabernacle → temple → Jesus → New Jerusalem

Following this theme reminds us of the blessed condition into which God initially placed humans. It rehearses the horrible condition of alienation from God's presence that was the result of our sin. It also shows God's relentless pursuit to restore us to harmonious relationship with him. It also communicates to us that, though we still live in the period before the New Jerusalem, there is no doubt as to the outcome. We will be restored to relationship with our God.

QUESTIONS FOR DISCUSSION

1. Summarize the reason(s) why the place where God made his presence known changed during the Old Testament time period.

2. What is the relationship between Jesus and the Old Testament holy places?

3. Many conservative Jewish people and even some Christians believe that the temple is going to be rebuilt in the future. Does this make sense in the light of the biblical theology of the presence of God? Why or why not?

FOR FURTHER READING

Poythress, V. *The Shadow of Christ in the Law of Moses*. Phillipsburg, N.J.: P & R, 1995.

Woudstra, M. *The Ark of the Covenant from Conquest to Kingship*. Philadelphia: Presbyterian and Reformed, 1965.

WHO WROTE
THE BOOK OF EXODUS?

The question of who wrote Exodus is important, but does not admit of an easy or simple answer. The authorship of Exodus is integrally connected to the authorship of the rest of the Torah, since it is part two of a five-part literary composition. I have relegated this discussion to an appendix for two reasons. First, I have treated the question of the authorship of the Pentateuch at length in my book *How to Read Genesis*, and have not substantially changed my views on the subject since that time. Those who have recently read that book may not need to read this summary statement. However, those who have not read that book may want to become acquainted with the issues. Readers who want an even more detailed treatment can also refer to the books and articles listed in the Further Reading section at the end of this appendix. Second, placing this discussion in the appendix allows me to concentrate on the final form in the body of the book. After all, no matter how the book came into existence, what is important for the Christian is the final canonical form.

What is at stake with this question? That is always a good consideration with which to begin a discussion of a topic. The most pointed issue involved is the status of Moses in the production of the Pentateuch. The traditional view says that Moses wrote the Pentateuch (usually with the qualifications noted below). The view that has become the mainstay of mainstream biblical scholarship argues that Moses had nothing to do with the Pentateuch. One might ask: "Who cares? The authority of the book comes from God, not Moses." While that is a pious answer, it does not reflect the biblical text itself. Yes, of course, the ultimate authority behind the Torah is God, but the Torah and the biblical books that follow invest Moses with a considerable measure of authority as well. Moses occupies a special place as a prophet in the Bible (Num 12:6-8; Deut 18:15-22; 34:10-12). The biblical text itself offers Moses as a source of authority.

Granting that, though, does not mean it is necessary to believe he wrote all of the Pentateuch. After all, as we observed in the section on the style of Exodus, much of it is written in third-person omniscient narrative. It is reporting what Moses did and said. Thus, what is truly important is that the Torah (including Exodus) preserves true traditions about Moses. To think, for instance, that later authors put forward the law on the authority of Moses and that we should nonetheless accept and observe them on the authority of God is difficult to assimilate theologically.

Again, this viewpoint does not mean that Moses wrote the entirety of the Pentateuch. What does Exodus itself say about its composition? Nowhere in Exodus or elsewhere in the Pentateuch do we have anything like a superscription that affirms Moses' authorship. The Pentateuch is technically anonymous. Even so, there are the occasional references to Moses writing things down that are included in the Pentateuch. In the book of Exodus we see two such places, both connected with the law. After receiving the law for the first time on Mount Sinai, the narrator tells us: "Then Moses carefully wrote down all the Lord's instructions" (Ex 24:4). After breaking the original tablets of the law, God tells Moses, "Write down all these instructions, for they represent the terms of the covenant I am making with you and with Israel" (Ex 34:27).

Of course, these verses do not provide the basis for thinking that Moses wrote the whole book of Exodus. Later inspired redactors could very well be responsible for the final form of the Pentateuch. Indeed, there are well-known postmosaica (passages that had to be written after Moses' death) in the Pentateuch, the most notable of which is the account of his death in Deuteronomy 34. These could be just the tip of the iceberg though. In my opinion, while it is important to preserve a connection between Moses and the tradition of the law, whether there is significant updating and supplementation by inspired redactors is theologically insignificant. Much of the Old Testament is written by anonymous authors and redactors.

Nonetheless, this view is considerably different from those which completely disconnect the Pentateuch from Moses. The classic articulation of the so-called Documentary Hypothesis does this by dating the earlier source J to the tenth century B.C. (see above for the dating of Moses in the fifteenth or thirteenth centuries). A full presentation of such alternative source-critical theories will not be presented here because of the earlier treatments mentioned above and cited below. Typical source critical studies of Exodus will comment on the presence of the J and E sources, though it is often observed that separating the two is difficult if not impossible. The same trouble pertains to P, which seems, according to these theories, tightly bound with the other sources. The legal material of Exodus is often thought to be independent of the sources. For those who wish to see how a typical modern source-critical analysis handles Exodus, see R. E. Friedman (*The Bible with Sources Revealed* [HarperSanFrancisco, 2003], pp. 119-89), where the suggested sources are all color-coded for ease of reference.

The view of this book though is that Exodus is rooted in the experience and writing of Moses. The prophet may have used sources and the evidence is clear that he did not bring the book to its final form. However, the focus of our interpretation should not be on the impossible task of differentiating Moses from later writing. Indeed, there is no need to do so because the faith of the church affirms that it is the final form of the book and not the specific words of Moses that are canonical.

FOR FURTHER READING

For those wishing a more developed presentation of my view see:

Longman, Tremper, III. *How to Read Genesis.* Downers Grove, Ill.: Inter-
Varsity Press, 2005, pp. 43-58.

Longman, Tremper, III, and Raymond B. Dillard. *An Introduction to the
Old Testament.* 2nd ed. Grand Rapids: Zondervan, 2006, pp. 40-53.

Also highly recommended:

Alexander, T. Desmond. *Abraham in the Negev: A Source Critical Investigation of Genesis 20:1-22:19.* Carlisle, U.K.: Paternoster, 1997.

———. "Authorship of the Pentateuch," pp. 61-72. In *Dictionary of the
Old Testament: Pentateuch,* edited by T. Desmond Alexander and David W. Baker. Downers Grove, Ill.: InterVarsity Press, 2003.

Baker, D. W. "Source Criticism," pp. 798-805. In *Dictionary of the Old
Testament: Pentateuch,* edited by T. Desmond Alexander and David W.
Baker. Downers Grove, Ill.: InterVarsity Press, 2003.

COMMENTARIES ON
THE BOOK OF EXODUS

The following are all excellent; which one you buy depends on what you are looking for, since not every commentary can address every aspect of the book. Also, the various commentaries come from different theological and methodological perspectives.

Cassuto, U. *Commentary on the Book of Exodus,* translated by I. Abrahams. Jerusalem: Magnes Press, 1967. Cassuto rejects the Documentary Hypothesis and explains the existing text. He is sensitive to the literary artistry of Exodus and brilliant in his philological analysis. See also comments under his commentary on Genesis.

Childs, B. S. *The Book of Exodus.* Old Testament Library. Philadelphia: Westminster Press, 1974. Childs divides his commentary into different sections, including textual criticism and philology, critical methods, Old Testament context, New Testament context and history of interpretation. Although representing a critical perspective, this volume is valuable to evangelical ministers.

Cole, R. Alan. *Exodus.* Tyndale Old Testament Commentaries. Downers Grove, Ill.: InterVarsity Press, 1973. As is the case with all the volumes in this series, this is a book with all the inherent disadvantages of a short commentary. There is not much on matters of general introduction or interaction with source criticism, but there is an excellent theological introduction. It is definitely worth the price.

Durham, J. I. *Exodus*. Word Biblical Commentary. Waco, Tex.: Word, 1987. The strength of this commentary is its focus on the theology of the text. Its weakness is its casual attitude toward the historicity of Exodus. Durham identifies the heart of the book's message as the presence of God with his people.

Ellison, H. L. *Exodus*. Daily Study Bible. Louisville: Westminster/John Knox, 1982. Ellison does a good job explaining the text to the modern lay reader. He is insightful, but the commentary is too brief. The introduction is short even for the series, and makes only passing reference to the critical problems of history. Ellison emphasizes theology and is committed to a New Testament approach after studying the text in its Old Testament context.

Enns, Peter. *Exodus*. New International Version Application Commentary. Grand Rapids: Zondervan, 2000. Enns has produced an incredibly insightful theological study of the book. He also deals well with the important historical issues, but not from a technical standpoint. This commentary is ideal for those preaching on the book because he so thoughtfully explores the book's trajectory toward the New Testament gospel.

Fretheim, Terence E. *Exodus*. Interpretation. Louisville: John Knox, 1991. This very readable volume is stimulating in terms of the theological message of the book of Exodus. Fretheim might be described as a moderate critic who concentrates on the final form of the text. This volume is not particularly helpful on the more technical aspects of the book.

Propp, W. H. C. *Exodus 1–18*. Anchor Bible. New York: Doubleday, 1998; idem. *Exodus 19–40*. Anchor Bible. New York: Doubleday, 2006. Propp's commentary has some unique features compared to other volumes in the series. For one thing, each section begins with a comment on the text, source and redaction criticism. Also, contrary to the practice of most biblical scholars, Propp marks a speculative remark as speculative (other scholars will judge that some of his un-marked comments are also speculative!). His opening translation is quite literal, even awkwardly so. Many readers will find these features a bit confusing and off-putting, but there are some excellent insights into the text in this commentary.

Sarna, N. M. *Exodus*. JPS Torah Commentary. Philadelphia: Jewish Publication Society, 1991. Sarna is one of the masters of commentary writing on the Torah. This volume is noticeably shorter than the others in the series and lacks their vitality. Nonetheless, the serious student should consult it.

Stuart, Douglas. *Exodus*. New American Commentary. Nashville: Broadman and Holman, 2006. A well-written exposition of the book from an evangelical perspective. One wishes for a more extensive reflection on the relationship between the theology of Exodus and the New Testament, but still many important insights.

Author Index

Subject Index

Scripture Index